# Praise for *Outloud*

Dealing with our past pain and trauma requires a tremendous amount of courage. We must be willing to step into our memories, trusting that God will guide us, carry us, and protect us from getting lost in despair. As a woman who has dealt with my own trauma while also walking alongside many other women, I am immensely thankful for Michele's willingness to share her story. God designed us to grow and heal through relationships with others. By sharing her journey with us, Michele's testimony is a guide and encouragement as we navigate the difficult parts of our stories.

*—Stacey Pardoe, author of* Lean Into Grace: Let God's Grace Heal Your Heart, Refresh Your Soul, and Set You Free *and writer at staceypardoe.com*

In *Outloud: The Sound of Healing—A Memoir Part II*, Michele Evette Vrabel continues the deeply moving journey she began in *Butterfly Stitches: The Metamorphosis of Healing*. With her signature vulnerability and spiritual insight, Michele invites readers once again into the sacred space of her healing story. Her words don't just tell a story—they offer hope, restoration, and the comforting reminder that healing is not a destination but a beautifully unfolding process. As someone who knows Michele and has walked alongside her in our mutual calling as authors, I'm honored to witness and support the impact of her work. This book is a gift to anyone seeking redemption through pain and purpose through trials.

*—Dawn R. Ward, author of* From Guilt to Grace: Hope and Healing for Christian Moms of Addicted Children

Reading Michele Vrabel's memoir *Outloud* took me on an emotional journey—filled with laughter, tears, and moments of righteous anger. Through her honest and heartfelt storytelling, Michele shares the deep hardships she's endured, all while clinging to her faith and embracing a spirit of hope. Her story is a powerful testament to God's ability to heal, restore, and transform brokenness into something beautiful. *Outloud* is ultimately a moving reflection on forgiveness, resilience, and the sustaining strength Michele found in Jesus Christ through life's most difficult storms.

—*Brianna Barrett, Author of* Hope in the Healing: A 40-Day Devotional Journey Through Chronic Illness.

Michele Vrabel's *Outloud* is her follow-up memoir to *Butterfly Stitches*. It delves into the heartbreaking wounds that once threatened to destroy her. Her deeply moving story offers a fresh and moving perspective on the healing process. In the pages of this book, Michele courageously chronicles the harrowing years of her 15-year abusive marriage and the miraculous healing that God guided her through. Her journey is a testament to the transformative power of the Holy Spirit. *Outloud* equips us with practical steps to navigate healing in the emotional, spiritual, mental, and physical realms, making us feel prepared to begin our own healing journey. Michele encourages us to submit to our King, Jesus, and "become what we were beautifully and wonderfully made to be."

—*Deborah Rutherford, Author of* Unexpected Blessings: 40 Days of Discovering God's Best

# Outloud

## The Sound
## OF HEALING

*a memoir*
PART II

michele evette vrabel

ISBN: 979-8-9908647-2-6 (print)

ISBN: 979-8-9908647-3-3 (eBook)

ISBN: 979-8-9908647-4-0 (*Outloud* Healing Companion—paperback)

Cover and book design by Melissa Williams Design

Photography by Lindsey Wheeler

# Contents

## Season IV: Reckoning

### *Emotional*

### *Spiritual*

### *Mental*

### *Physical*

## The Sound of Healing

### *Emotional*

### *Spiritual*

# Foreword

## The Year of the Lord's Favor

61 The Spirit of the Sovereign Lord is on me,
    because the Lord has anointed me
    to proclaim good news to the poor.
He has sent me to bind up the brokenhearted,
    to proclaim freedom for the captives
and release from darkness for the prisoners,
    2 to proclaim the year of the Lord's favor
    and the day of vengeance of our God,
        to comfort all who mourn,
3   and provide for those who grieve in Zion—
    to bestow on them a crown of beauty
            instead of ashes,
            the oil of joy
        instead of mourning,
        and a garment of praise
        instead of a spirit of despair.
They will be called oaks of righteousness,
        a planting of the Lord
    for the display of his splendor.
4 They will rebuild the ancient ruins
    and restore the places long devastated;
    they will renew the ruined cities
that have been devastated for generations.
5 Strangers will shepherd your flocks;
foreigners will work your fields and vineyards.
6 And you will be called priests of the Lord,
    you will be named ministers of our God.
You will feed on the wealth of nations,
    and in their riches you will boast.
        7 Instead of your shame
    you will receive a double portion,

and instead of disgrace
you will rejoice in your inheritance.
And so you will inherit a double portion in your land,
and everlasting joy will be yours.
8 "For I, the Lord, love justice;
I hate robbery and wrongdoing.
In my faithfulness I will reward my people
and make an everlasting covenant with them.
9 Their descendants will be known among the nations
and their offspring among the peoples.
All who see them will acknowledge
that they are a people the Lord has blessed."
10 I delight greatly in the Lord;
my soul rejoices in my God.
For he has clothed me with garments of salvation
and arrayed me in a robe of his righteousness,
as a bridegroom adorns his head like a priest,
and as a bride adorns herself with her jewels.
11 For as the soil makes the sprout come up
and a garden causes seeds to grow,
so the Sovereign Lord will make righteousness
and praise spring up before all nations.
Isaiah 61 New International Version of the Holy Bible (NIV)


-ABBA FATHER, KING JESUS, HOLY SPIRIT

# Introduction

Out of the ashes . . . after the fire . . . the burning down of the life I thought I wanted or at the very least would be the life I had to endure until death . . . my King, my Jesus brought me up like no phoenix ever known. He truly gives beauty for ashes . . . strength for fear . . . gladness for mourning . . . peace for despair.

This was not a moment in time. This has been a several-year struggle to lay down my "rights." My right to know why. My right to fairness and justice. My right to security. My right to peace. My right to feel no pain.

My Savior and King showed me, held me, walked me through the hottest fire, the highest waters, the most hopeless moments and taught me that I truly do not want what I deserve or perceive to be "my rights." I fell desperately in love with my King all over again. He showed me that what He has for me is so much more than I could ever ask or imagine and that the need to understand anything that happened to me was so inconsequential in comparison to what I was made for and what He has for me.

It was not a snap of a finger; it was hard work. It was gut-wrenching, laying on the floor crying out, "Why? Please take this cup from me" kind of stuff. For the first time in my life, since my salvation, I totally submitted to the will of my Savior, and it was like a tumor I had carried my whole life was removed without anesthesia.

But, oh, the realization of the pain I had let myself become accustomed to, being taken away. I make no joke or churchy platitude here. Therefore, I feel compelled to share my journey. This, right here, if you take nothing else from this story . . . let it go . . . let go of your perceived right. Submit to what you are designed to be. Become what you were beautifully and wonderfully made to be.

It does not involve renouncing your worth. Instead, it is picking up the mantle of your worth. It does not involve renouncing your gender. Being a woman is unique; life-giving and has such monumental worth in the eyes of God that we are created to mother all life. It does not involve renouncing control over your life to any earthly being. It means you become the whole God-glorifying person you were meant to be so you would then be completely prepared for "the king."

I do not want my divorce or any other individual incident to define me. It is the course of a lifetime, the journey that got me here. Circumstances where I listened and was obedient, and sometimes, not so much. I wish I could let you touch my face like Spock from *Star Trek* and get the emotions, the full weight of what I walked through to get here. We do not all go through the same processes and yet we end up in the same place.

This is about the brokenness to let go of me and surrender to the peace that is real. Seriously, like a weight was removed from your shoulders and you can now let the King share your yoke and make your burden light. I seriously was whining and crying out daily to not have to go through some of the stuff I went through. But, if not for all of it, I would not be here.

You must decide that whatever you are going through, it will not be what defines you, nor is it what your purpose in life will be. No one . . . NO ONE . . . is promising you puppies and rainbows. The fact of the matter is that our decisions have consequences, and we need to be willing to acknowledge them and own them. Then we can move on to the right choices and the consequences that come with those.

I do not know the form they will take for you. For me, the most outstanding feature was peace that truly passed all understanding. Not only did I experience this, but my daughter brought to my attention how—for the first time—our home seemed so peaceful and joyful. Not perfect; she and I still had a lot of emotional and spiritual work to get us closer to whole, but nonetheless we were walking out of the furnace with King Jesus at our side.

As with *Butterfly Stitches*, the memoir part one, my story is told from the perspective of the emotional, spiritual, mental, and physical wounds I received during this season.

# Season IV

## RECKONING

# Chapter 1

## Conditional Love

---

"Nothing on earth hurts my soul deeper than
conditional love."

*–Brooke Bida*

---

He climbed onto the stationary bike next to me and asked,
"How are you doing?" His words started a conversation and
got my attention. I was seeing someone at the time and considered it nothing more than polite conversation. It became a
kind of routine for him to find me on the bike every day that I
worked out. He did not appear to be interested in more than
conversation.

The bodybuilder I was seeing had been attempting to manipulate me by saying all the right things to keep me hanging
around, while having a live-in girlfriend. For the first time ever,

I saw the situation for what it was and got out on my own terms.

The gym was buzzing about an upcoming bodybuilding competition that several members were entering. My bike buddy, Ray, had already entered a competition in Tucson and was not going to do another back-to-back, but he would be attending this one. He invited me to see him compete, but I had plans, and I was not thinking about dating anyone that young, since he was twenty-one and I was twenty-six at the time.

I decided to go to the competition in Phoenix with a girl-friend because there were a couple of guys from the gym who had caught my eye and there was a party afterward that might afford the opportunity to get to know them. We ran into Ray and one of his gym buddies at the show and discovered we were all going to the after-party.

At the party, I did get the opportunity to talk to men of interest; however, it turned out they were in relationships. My girlfriend and I ended up sitting in a group that included my new friend and his buddy. After a couple of hours talking, he offered to walk me to my car. He was well-built and attractive and appeared to determine that so was I. We "made out," and that was the auspicious start to my relationship with my future husband.

I was still not walking in relationship with God, and none of my decisions were in concert with prayer or the mind of Christ. I did not pray about or ask my Jesus if I should even be in a relationship at all, let alone moving in together and plowing forward at full steam. I was functioning in protection mode and was making decisions by my "feels." Which is ex-tremely ironic considering that during the time I was dating my future husband, I allowed and forgave things that my younger self would never have allowed to happen. I was, however, still an extremely vulnerable and unloved woman. It amazed me how people, not only men, can smell vulnerability on you. The signs that this would not be a monogamous and faithful relationship were numerous, even before the wedding bells.

\* \* \*

We had a routine that included going out on Friday nights where he would go with the fellas and I with my girlfriends, and then we would all meet at a club later. One Friday, there was going to be a bachelor party for one of the guys, and so they were headed to a strip club. We all met up as usual, and there was no evidence that things were worse for wear because of these shenanigans.

I was preparing for a bodybuilding competition that was approximately three months away. Ray came out of the bedroom dressed to go out and indicated that he was meeting his friend at a bar and going to a movie. I liked the particular friend and thought nothing of them doing stuff together. I believe people until they give me a reason not to.

He was not gone for ten minutes when I got a phone call on our apartment's landline. A woman's voice asked for Ray, and when I asked what this was regarding, she said she was running late and wanted to let him know. I asked who she was, and she said she was a stripper from the club the previous weekend that he had approached and asked out. She asked who I was and went ballistic once she knew I was his live-in girlfriend. She told me to meet her at the bar he had chosen so we could "surprise" him. I called a friend and asked her to come to the parking lot in case I was too shook up to drive or to keep me from going off the deep end.

During the whole drive, I hoped that this was not real. His car was in the parking lot and my heart sank. As I walked into the bar, he was sitting holding a beer and his feet were up on the chair next to him. He nonchalantly said, "Hey" as I got closer. I was visibly shaking as my heart was breaking once again and felt like a familiar wound was being reopened. I asked where his friend was, and he said that he had not arrived yet. I asked, "Do you really want to do this in here?"

He got up slowly and followed me outside. When I heard the door fall shut, I spun around with my arm fully extended and slapped him across the face. He put his hands up to block as I pummeled him with slaps and punches to the face while telling him what I knew. To his credit, he did not strike back. He did not answer me or give an explanation. He did not apologize. I kept hitting him. At one point, he grabbed both my wrists and asked if I was finished. I said yes, he let go, and I started over.

He continued his vow of silence which only added to my pain. The stripper never showed up. My friend watched and was satisfied that I was not going overboard for Ray's infraction. I told him to get his shit from the apartment the next day, or he would find it on the lawn. I cried all the way back home. Sprawled on the bed, I laid there thinking, *How could this be happening to me again?*

We had only been together a few months and having moved in together; it seemed we were on good footing. What had been the cause of the lying and choice to cheat? I realize this relationship would not be a desirable choice for me no matter who, as I had not genuinely healed from my last devastating relationship when I was living in Hawaii. This did not feel like something I had done wrong, as opposed to his particular *modus operandi.*

When he came the next day to get his things, he was contrite. I received one of only a couple of apologies I would ever get from him, and I am not sure it was real. He still gave no explanation, and I am honestly not sure why I asked. When someone does something this dishonest, do I really believe I would have gotten the truth anyway? His ability to choose his words carefully, manipulate the target of his attention, and make others feel sorry for him were skills that would serve him, and him alone, well in the future. Along with whatever else he said, this got him back in the apartment and further access to my already-wounded heart.

We lived together for eight years, moved to California and back to Arizona, and opened businesses together. During that time, multiple incidents of Ray's unfaithfulness occurred. Still, I persevered. Not even consciously knowing why. Perhaps some desire to see someone who had indicated they loved me follow through. We had four thriving General Nutrition Center franchises, and we bought a house together. I suppose getting married was the next right thing to do more than some sort of "soulmate" decision.

We had separated the year before our engagement over an "extra-relationship situation." It felt like my old wounds that had barely scabbed over were being torn open all over again. Nonetheless, the wedding went forward. One of the participants in the extracurriculars of my groom was invited to our wedding, unbeknownst to me.

\* \* \*

Our first two years of marriage were a mixed bag. If he was unfaithful, he was better at hiding it, at least for a little while. We were also trying to get pregnant, which required him to be more present with me. We were battling for our lives with our businesses. The parent corporation had made some decisions that did not fare well for their franchisees and were wreaking havoc on finances. The stress was incredible and was not well-tolerated by my body. We were going through all the traditional testing to see if we had any fertility issues. My cycle was like clockwork, and due to his previous use of steroids for bodybuilding, the doctors assumed that looking at him was our first step.

The results were disheartening, since I was in my late thirties, and everyone was treating me like I was a mummy or a sarcophagus. As we got further into the battle for our business, we had to take a hard look at finances and determine when the war was over for us. In March, 2000, we made the decision to close our last remaining franchise. We had both gotten outside jobs in preparation and had warned our staff to do the same.

The day we walked away and closed the store, I felt as if I had the flu and cried for the next two days. The weather had been bad, and I felt like my sickness had moved to a sinus infection. I went to the doctor to get tested and get some relief. Since my doctor knew we were trying to start a family, she did a pregnancy test to be safe before administering meds. After I performed the lovely ritual of peeing in a cup, the nurse ushered me back to the exam room for the wait. She came in and said the tests were positive. I was thinking of my sinus infection because it felt like two monkeys were having a cage match inside my skull.

She started crying for me and took me by the shoulders and informed me that I was going to be a momma. Me. God chose me. I understood completely why I could not continue under the stress and strain of the battle for our business if I were going to bring forth a life and survive it all.

My pregnancy was uneventful regarding any relationship trauma at home. Despite my advanced age, we made it through all the pregnancy milestones, and no medical interventions were required. Both our families as well as our church family came together for a wonderful baby shower that was over-the-top and provided diapers for the first two years of our baby's life.

On Monday, November 13th, 2000, at 11:59 p.m., I got to meet my precious Peanut. Birthing Maya Victoria took twenty-three hours of hard labor, but once we got down to it, she popped out without a hitch. If I had created a list for God, it would not have been even half of what He chose to give me in this beautiful creature.

After all that had happened to me. After all the choices I had made. I was given the honor of being her momma. I cried uncontrollably at the galactic joy I received. We have been shown by our Abba Father the unconditional love that we can turn around and give to other humans, especially those we give birth to.

\* \* \*

After being in a bassinet in our room for several months, Maya was moved to her own room. Ray would come to find me standing over her like a zombie from lack of sleep. Almighty God is love and grace. I do not believe that He would have taken her. I did believe, unrealistically, that due to my choice to have an abortion when I was younger, my consequences might be losing her. She had eczema and breathing issues, and Sudden Infant Death Syndrome (SIDS) was a real danger. My heart hurt for the choices I had made in the past, and I was terrified that it would have generational consequences.

A nurse in my Bible study at church heard my story. She came to me and was incredibly kind and practical. She told me that even if I were standing over my baby, I would not be able to do anything about it if in fact SIDS happened. While this information was disheartening, it was also a relief. I had to put my little Peanut in God's hands and let us both get some sleep.

\* \* \*

Sadly, it was within her first year of life that the extramarital affair that would end my marriage began. My husband had begun working as a personal trainer while we were winding down our business in preparation for closing. After about a year of that, he decided to go into business for himself as a muralist and specialty finish painter. Without talking to me, he hired one of his female training clients to assist him in our business. We had an agreement that he would be an all-male company with me as the sole female overseeing the business administration.

At first, I agreed to see how things went. It did not take long for them to need to meet outside of business hours to do "project management." They would spend the day together and then need to meet someplace for dinner and further discussion. This became routine several nights a week, and because of our history, had an extremely specific feel to it. I told him the after-hours meetings needed to stop, and his anger and defensiveness were extreme for the situation, if all of this was aboveboard.

He told me if I wanted her gone, I would have to let her go. I sent her an email explaining how, as a Christian company, we wanted to be above impropriety and that for both her marriage and ours, this would be best. She came unhinged. She claimed that my husband was "her light and connection to Jesus" and that I could not do this. She was frantic. I explained to her that no man should be her connection to Jesus, but even if that were so, it should be her own husband. This is where she began to unravel and never recovered.

For the first round of marriage counseling, Ray made the appearance of wanting reconciliation. It was, however, never a reality. He was a very sympathetic character in our drama.

Every single set of counselors felt so sorry for him. The focus was always that I needed to be more forgiving. No real need for him to repent and stop what he was doing. So, he did not.

In the beginning, I naively believed that the affair had not been physical yet. He swore up and down, and I had no evidence. One fateful morning, he left his cell phone at home. It was blowing up, and I figured he needed it for work. I had never looked at his phone, even while all of this was happening. Well, I looked that day because of clients possibly reaching out. Every single one of the dozens of texts was from her. Wondering where he was and sending naked pictures of herself from her bedroom at her home where she lived with her husband and kids.

Without pausing to calm down, I decided to be a good wife and take him his phone. When I got to the jobsite, he saw me and began walking toward me, smiling. I pitched the phone at him, aiming at his head. He ducked, and the phone hit a concrete wall and was smashed to bits. I informed him of what I saw. He feigned shock and tried to act confused. I told him where he could put that. I said I did not care where he went but he was not staying in our house that night and that he could get his crap while our ten-year-old daughter was not home and come back to be the one to explain to her why he was leaving.

\* \* \*

He moved into a hotel near our house, claiming he wanted to be near our daughter. That way, he would not have to stay with his mom and hear her thoughts on the matter. He came back to the house after a few days to talk to Maya. I did not expect him to be explicit; however, in my opinion he took the easy way out, telling her, "Daddy made a mistake."

We started another round of counseling with a Christian

couple from our church who indicated they had training in marriage counseling. It started as it always had with my husband painting a very sympathetic picture of himself, and the counselors believing him hook, line, and sinker. I, too, chose to put my heart back on the line and try some more.

We met with our counselors every other week, but we were given a DVD set by Bruce Wilkerson called *A Biblical Portrait of Marriage* to watch weekly at home, which exposed some very raw insights for the both of us. During one session on leading, we were more honest and transparent with one another than we had been in our entire relationship. One nugget in particular was that we both acknowledged that after eight years together, owning four businesses and a house, that getting married was more about taking what seemed like the next logical step, versus being about a "love of my life" decision.

Instead of this making either one of us feel bad, you could visibly see a type of peace come over us. It was not manipulation, and I truly felt a different energy in giving my marriage more time. It is the only time in all the struggle and infidelity that I felt Ray was also trying. I had him come to speak to our daughter about what was happening and the reason he would now be moving back home. He told her, "Daddy made a mistake and won't see this other woman, and he loves you and mommy more." Because of the latest session and couples Bible study, and the effort that seemed genuine in the beginning, I felt hopeful.

Over the next few years, my daughter and I traveled extensively for both homeschooling and mission trips with our church. When we returned home, there were signs of someone else having been in our home. The counselors had us do everything from getting the woman on the phone and having Ray tell her it was over and to stop contacting him, to of course me forgiving him publicly even though he never apologized or repented.

On a friend's advice, I tried to prepare myself for the eventuality that I would have to have resources and be on my own with my daughter. I decided not to point out every time I saw evidence of the other woman's return. I do not believe it was an accident that she chose to send naked pics of herself again after our latest round of me telling a supposedly "Christian" woman to stand down and go home to her husband. MY husband was clearly participating.

\* \* \*

The very last round of counseling broke me. The couple had been our counselors for several rounds. While Ray never apologized, he had never accused me of cheating, and I had, in fact, never cheated on him. Not once had they ever focused on his repentance. They were constantly pressing me to forgive him. Pressing me as to providing for his needs.

On this occasion, it looked as if they were finally going to address him, the adulterer. He decided to throw out a grenade and say that seventeen years earlier I had gotten with one of our customers at our GNC stores.

I was speechless. I had no idea what his play was here, other than diversion. Well, the counselors took the bait. The two of them went off on me. How could I sit here and not forgive him if I had, in fact, myself cheated? I was not asked if I had. The fact that he had been unfaithful to me for fifteen years and used this tactic for the first time now did not dissuade them. It was as if they could not bring themselves to truly "counsel" him regarding his behavior, and his accusations gave them an out.

They sat across the dining table from me, in my own home, with Ray at the end of the table. The husband rounded the table got inches from my face and started yelling at the top of his voice about what my infidelity was doing to "this man." Tears were streaming down my face. My husband had a slight smirk on his. Any desire to fight. Any desire to save my family . . . died that day. I do not remember what happened to make them finally go away, but, in my heart, I had decided to begin to prepare myself and my daughter to leave.

# Chapter 2

## Til Death Do Us Part

"I've never considered divorce," she said once.
"Murder, yes, but not divorce."

*–Ruth Bell Graham*

Three days after one of the saddest Christmases I have ever had, it happened. I got my daughter situated with breakfast at home and left to meet Ray at our business to head out to do some estimates for painting jobs. When I walked into the shop . . . there it was. A simple phone charging on the counter. This phone had popped up months earlier and had been dismissed with a lie. I was defeated and had decided not to give him a heads-up about my plans, and I just functioned as if I was oblivious to all the signs of their involvement.

He must have thought I was not coming in until a bit later

because he looked stunned and glanced over at the phone. Even though I knew, I asked, "Is that for her?" He said no and stood looking at me defiantly. I said, "Nothing can be worse than what I already know. Can't you please just once tell the truth?" He conceded that the phone was in fact for her. I told him it was over. I said, "I forgive you because I cannot hang onto this any longer, but it is over." I told him to get his things out of the house when our daughter was not home and reach out about when he could come and explain to her.

He did not try to apologize or stop me. I left and cried all the way home. More out of relief than sadness. My marriage had been over before it began. I was sitting and crying in my car parked on the street in our neighborhood when his truck went by, despite my telling him to wait. We ended up in the house at the same time when he decided to address our daughter, and he began his story, unhappy that I was there.

He tried the same "Daddy has made a mistake" routine he had performed years earlier, but our daughter was fifteen now and called him on his bullshit. He kept trying to blather on, and she kept asking, "Is it the same woman?" "Is it the same woman?" Finally, he said yes. Tears were streaming down her face as she walked off and slammed her door. He took some clothes and checked into the same hotel as before.

\* \* \*

I cried for three days. Not because I wanted him to want me or to come back. Because finally losing what I had been fighting to save felt like a death in the family. My daughter went back and forth between being mad at all of us and coming to the couch where I was quietly crying and laying her head in my lap and joining me. She was genuinely devastated and mad at her dad. She decided to share her thoughts on the part I played in her heart breaking. Because I had not told her how terrible things were, she felt I had lied as well. She was not wrong. I explained that I thought I was protecting her, and I was in denial about my marriage being at the breaking point.

After a couple of weeks of ridiculous conversations over the phone about things that I used to do as his wife and partner in our business, I finally agreed to a face-to-face discussion. He graciously felt that if everything stayed the same, except he would be living somewhere else, it would be best for us all. He would pay the house bills, and I could ask for an allowance. He expected me to continue to work with him so he could control my time and his money.

My rebuttal was that we ask trusted friends to mediate, and we try to get something official on paper on our own, without lawyers. He loved the "without lawyers" thought process. Something "official" was another story altogether. Reluctantly, he agreed, and we set the first meeting. We went to church with a couple that agreed to help us, and so we chose to meet in our small group room to keep things neutral.

I had helped him start and grow this business for seventeen years and had not taken a single paycheck. We took draws to pay the bills. Our money arrangement while married was that I could not spend more than $100 without a conversation with him, and so he believed that all I needed in the divorce was the bills paid for the house, and I could come and ask him if I needed anything beyond that.

The truth of the matter was that his business was his first mistress and the other woman was the second. Selling our daughter's only home was not an issue for him regarding split-ting assets. Selling his business or me getting any of it was, in his mind, not going to happen. He did not feel I deserved alimony, and he rejected five different proposals from me as to how to amicably end our marriage. I thought the adultery was horrific, but I had not seen anything yet.

Having reached an impasse, he requested a visit to our home to discuss the latest proposal. Shortly after his arrival, it became clear that he had no interest in discussing anything. I was to listen to how it was going to go and accept it. He knew about the physical and verbal abuse in my background and chose to raise his voice for effect anyway. I had been literally broken for the last time and probably looked slightly amused at the caricature he portrayed.

After I informed him that I did not find his terms acceptable, he stood up, leaned across the table in my direction, and started yelling. He was going to take all our money and get a lawyer, and then I would see what would happen. I waited for him to leave before crying, since I did not want him to feel he had won.

Seeing that our mediation with friends was not bearing fruit, I had asked some other friends for lawyer recommendations and had a couple of numbers. It was a Friday night at about 6:30 p.m., and I decided I would at least leave a message. The lawyer called me back within ten minutes. I was still shaking and told her I had not expected a call so quickly. She said, "You sounded like you needed it."

She explained the legalities of what could be done with "our" money and how I needed to handle myself. I went to the bank the next morning and was there when they unlocked the doors. As long as between accounts we had equal amounts, I could secure money in another dedicated account. The money had to be used for me to survive, not to go on vacation. I was shaking and crying, and a dear friend was waiting for me when I returned home. She recommended a lock change for the house, and I believe between that and the bank, it was the shot heard 'round the world.

* * *

Once again, I made my own choices, and while I had returned to a right relationship with God, I did choose to marry without even so much as a prayer as to whether this was His will for my life. My ex made the choice to commit adultery, and that is on him, but I made the choice to forgive and stay in our marriage. Perhaps too long.

In any case, I cannot change the past and my journey to emotional health had its best foundations in the time during and following the fire of the furnace of my divorce. I do not wish to be defined by any of the things that happened to me at the hands of men who were supposed to love me. But they are definitely things that were instrumental in shaping my ability to recover and make healthy choices going forward. They have shaped and irrevocably altered my emotional intelligence, and I will take that forward in whatever form and learn and grow from it.

I have struggled with the desire to be needed and for the attention of someone who values me. The funny thing is that I have accepted the attention of narcissists with a sexualized agenda for the sake of any attention at all. I have lost the vision of my own value, and part of my journey is getting that back. What my true King taught me going through these trials is my journey . . . my preparation for my king . . . my story.

# Chapter 3

## Welcome Home

> "A man travels the world over in search of what he needs and returns home to find it."
>
> *–George Moore*

I met my future husband at the gym, and this would be pivotal for many things in my spiritual journey. My ten-year hiatus from my relationship with my Savior was nearing its end. I was still making decisions that were what I thought was protective. I entered a relationship with my future husband, and there were red flags out of the starting gate.

He asked for exclusivity in our relationship and almost immediately went on a date with another bodybuilder from our gym. I cannot for the life of me pinpoint the moment when I let my guard down and decided to tolerate the kind of behavior that was clearly focusing on infidelity for him. There was nothing significantly different or special about him that separated him from other guys I had dated and cast aside for similar behavior.

He came from a Catholic background, and we did take our mothers to Christmas and Easter mass, as they were both devout. Despite my unfortunate history with the Catholic Church, the Holy Spirit used these events to get my attention. I was irritated by all the elements that had been a part of the church and the priest who had shut the door in our faces; it was salt in an old wound that had not fully healed.

After buying our home and getting settled, while still just living together, I began to feel anxious. We may have been "playing house" but we were only engaged, not married yet, and this was not a home that I had prayed about or received the blessing of my King to move forward with.

I started feeling the Holy Spirit drawing me to get back into fellowship with both God and a church family. I started visiting churches near our home and prayed fervently about where I should be. I was very emotional and crying a lot during this time, and my fiancé was concerned that I was changing my mind about him.

When I told him what I was doing, he stopped asking and never chose to come with me when I attended church. Even after all we had been through, I had still not prayed about him, for him, or about whether he was the man God had for me. I had not prayed about whether I should be in a relationship with him at all. This isn't an excuse for his behavior, but it's the reason I cannot plop all our relationship angst in his lap.

I visited several churches and was led to join a Baptist church close to our home where the community reminded me of my church back in Decatur, Michigan. The pastor stayed

21

true to sound doctrine and had a great sense of humor, which works well for me. It was a small congregation, and several ladies made me feel at home right away.

I decided to join a ladies' Bible study group, and this would mean that two days a week I was leaving the house for church. It seemed to annoy Ray that I suddenly needed to attend church. I believe it was the Holy Spirit convicting him of his need to be in relationship with Jesus.

The wedding planning finally started, and the date was set. Ray did agree upon a pastor to marry us, although we got married at a resort and not in the church. The gentleman who married us was a customer at our GNC store, and he had been a military chaplain. He was strict and wanted to know whether we would either meet with him or assure him we had pre-marital counseling.

Chaplain Joe met with us several times and gave some very good advice as well as praying over us each time. This satisfied him to move forward with the nuptials. The ladies in my Bible study were concerned, since they knew I would be unequally yoked, and that is an inauspicious beginning to any relationship. They had been praying for Ray from the moment I had joined the church.

\* \* \*

The first two years of our marriage were very trying, and the situation was about to come to loggerheads when something only my Jesus could do happened. Ray asked to come to church with me. To say I was speechless was an understatement. I had been praying for my marriage and for the ability to see how it could be healed and move forward in the plans God had for us, despite my not having asked Him what they were in the first place.

This was a new experience for my husband, since Baptist churches and Catholic churches do not operate the same way. The pastor telling us to "turn to_____ in the Bible" was something that had not happened in his church-attending lifetime. Ray saw my devotion to my Bible study each morning as I would go into our spare bedroom to do my lessons. He began to bring me a cup of coffee regularly, stating he wanted me to be able to focus on what I was doing.

There was a little more peace in our home, and that was a blessing all its own. Several months of church attendance together went by when all the prayers of the ladies in my Bible study group bore fruit. My husband had been asking questions of me and some of the men in the church and apparently made a decision. He simply turned to me during the invitation one Sunday and went forward and made the decision to get saved. There was not a dry eye in the place.

The husband of one of the ladies in my Bible study offered to mentor him, and that went well for a while. He went on the men's retreat at our church and with several of the men to the Promise Keepers conference. He started to begin his day with Bible study and coffee as well.

Just because my husband had begun a relationship with my Jesus, I did not believe that everything in our marriage would automatically be sunshine and cupcakes. That is not how salvation works. Our relationship with Jesus helps us to grow through experiences to be more like him. We are still in this world, and healing and learning from our previous choices is a process.

I did, however, believe that his relationship with Jesus would motivate Ray to make better choices in regard to our relationship. It genuinely seemed as if he were making life choices that would bring honor to both God and to himself.

He stopped doing some things that are his story to tell, but that showed who he was, choosing to make Jesus his Lord and Savior. He had our sister-in-law, who was a graphic artist, create a brochure and other graphics for the business that declared that our business would be Christ-centered and above impropriety.

For a time, he and his crew would pray before starting a job or during lunch. All the young men who worked for us in the beginning were from the Bible college on our church campus, and that made for an environment for our clients that was God-honoring and integrity-filled.

I believe we had been unable to conceive because God knew that until my husband and I were in right relationship with Him and ourselves, we were not ready. Again, I enlisted the prayer warriors in my ladies' Bible study group. Not only that I might get to be a momma, but that our home life would remain stable as well.

I had chatted with a young lady at church who was working in several ministries. One of them was working with a lawyer who represented a Christian adoption agency. She gave me the lawyer's business card, and I had it in my back pocket the day I went to the doctor about my sinuses and learned that I was already going to be a momma.

We remained faithful to our Bible study and prayer times, in spite of horrible morning sickness for me. I do not believe that my salvation and relationship with Jesus is conditional. But I do believe we can have consequences for our sin, and sometimes they can be generational.

What I had done, I had repented and asked forgiveness for. Still. When I was sixteen, I had accidentally gotten pregnant and had murdered my first child. It hurt my soul. Did I deserve this child? Was I the reason we had a struggle getting here in the first place? I wanted peace so as not to fret myself into trouble with my "mature" pregnancy. None of this worry was rational or from the Lord. My sin and shame being brought to mind over and over were the defeatist tactics of Satan himself. He may have lost the battle for my soul, but perhaps he could render me ineffective again.

My beautiful baby girl, Maya Victoria, arrived four days late but one hundred percent perfect. There was Jesus. I was now a momma. Her love, like my King, was a balm for my soul that would be an anchor for our relationship.

The outpouring of love for our family and the arrival of my baby girl was an overwhelming blessing that made my soul sing. We had prayed for her and had a whole team of warriors doing the same. She was an answer to our prayers and the love of my life from the start.

* * *

The abortion I had had as a teenager when an older man had gotten me pregnant was a wound to my soul that had never healed. It was present and very real, every single day. I took how I was feeling before the Lord every morning in my prayer time and claimed the new mercies He had for me every day. It was not healing expeditiously.

As part of our women's ministry, the ladies in my Bible study went to a conference at a local megachurch. They always have breakout sessions and booths that represent the types of concerns we have as women and mothers. On this occasion, there was a booth that drew me in with the title "Pathway to Peace." As I approached the table, I could see that the terminology written in the literature was directed toward women who had had an abortion. I was the only one at the table, and yet

I felt as if the whole world's eyes were upon me and everyone knew what I had done.

This made me guarded and hesitant to engage when the woman behind the table greeted me. She told me that we did not need to speak at length now, but that she would call me and we could discuss whether this group would be a good fit for me. I gave her my number and times I would be available and went back to the main session. Uneasy about how that conversation would go, I thought about her the remainder of the weekend and until she called on Monday night.

She was direct and yet put me at ease at the same time. She indicated that she had to be cautious about who she allowed in the group because some protestors had infiltrated a couple of times and put everyone in danger. Because of my feelings re-emerging after my daughter was born, regarding the abortion I had, everything she said resonated with me.

I decided to join the group with an incredible amount of apprehension and the plan to depart should I get uncomfortable. Every bit of this group made me feel uncomfortable. Not because of the woman leading us or the ladies involved. It was my discomfort. Mine to own. It took the form of shame, guilt, and the desire to withdraw. This particular wound had been gaping since my junior year of high school. I had never dealt with it. I had repressed it, exactly as I had all the trauma of a lifetime.

She walked me through not only the trauma of the abortion itself, but also that of the sexual immorality associated with it. That had been a part of my entire life up to and including living with my husband before marriage and the infidelity of each and every one of the male participants.

My heart and soul were aching as we were coming to the conclusion of the group. Our last assignment was to write a letter forgiving ourselves. I said "no" abruptly and outloud. I got up, pointed at the leader, told her this was not going to happen, and walked out. I am not really sure why I had such a visceral reaction. I cried all the way home. She did not call or reach out to me. This was not her first rodeo, and she knew what she was doing.

As my colorful grandma would have said, the Holy Spirit "jerked a knot in my tail." Everywhere I turned, His word was coming up telling me if I do not forgive, I will not be forgiven. Not that we can lose our salvation; that would never happen. But my relationship with my King would be broken. I sat down with pen and paper and did not stop crying as I wrote eight pages, front and back.

I walked into the last night session of our group, and the leader was not surprised. She embraced me, and I cried uncontrollably the remainder of the night. She was having us read our letters outloud, and she purposefully had me go last. Upon hearing this, I was truly tempted to leave again. My time came, and all eyes were on me. By the grace of the Holy Spirit giving me the words that would start the healing, I read my entire letter with tears streaming down not only my cheeks, but those of everyone in the room.

We had a meal together and released balloons to celebrate the lives of our babies. I felt like I'd had a tumor removed without anesthesia. I went home and slept, totally exhausted, for two days. My Jesus never left me. He has genuinely never allowed this to be brought to my attention again, except as an offering to someone who might need it to work together for good.

# Chapter 4

## Through the Fire

---

"When you walk through the fire, you will not be
burned; the flames will not set you ablaze."

*–Isaiah 43:2a (NIV)*

---

While my husband's extracurriculars were ramping up during
this time, we still attended church as a family, and he appeared,
for now, to be invested in us. It did not go unnoticed by me
as a child that my father had been aggressive in our need to
attend church as a family, every Sunday, all while cheating on
my mom and beating us regularly.

The decision to hire the woman who would be instrumental
in the ultimate demise of our marriage came out of the blue. Or
at least I thought so. The business seemed to be doing well, and
customers were even commenting on how thrilled they were

with the godly young men who worked for us and the integrity with which we operated. If Ray had been carrying on with her all this time, he did a good job of covering it up, until he didn't.

It is not a calling on my life to judge. That is for King Jesus. He is fair and just. I am called to "love my neighbor as myself." No one who had said he loved me seemed to have ever meant it. Rejection and lying were more in line with their commitments. My soul needed someone to follow through. My Lord and Savior was the only one that this expectation could be placed upon.

Some friends of mine had their children attending a Christian school near our church and home, and I decided to check it out as a place for my daughter when she started school, so I could work part time at least. They had a school system from pre-K through high school and even a Bible college on the campus.

The preschool allowed for flexible hours, so this was a great opportunity to have Maya somewhere I felt safe leaving her and allowed me to work in our business doing estimates. My prayer was that this would fill the gap that my husband was trying to fill with the other woman. Also, because we went on estimates for our business together frequently, putting Maya in preschool allowed our relationship to stabilize as well.

Ray had hired more men to work in the shop and on jobsites who did not share our faith worldview. This changed the dynamic of our business, and some of the godly young men who worked for us decided to take their Bible college degrees and work elsewhere. Our customers were still delighted with our work, and the problem was not that we lost integrity in our reputation as a business. It became an environment where God was not at the center. Money now held that position.

We attended church weekly as a family. However, after

a Sunday afternoon nap, my husband began needing to do errands for work regularly. At first, I thought nothing of it, but when signs of another woman's presence became more apparent, my anxiety level rose. It was not long before Ray put little effort into covering up her reaching out and his accepting her advances.

Several more rounds of counseling ensued with Christian counselors. My soul hurt for how little hope I would receive from any of the sessions. He did muster up enough manipulation to make a good show, and the counselors would impress upon me that I must forgive and keep trying, each and every time. It is funny that people would ask me why I stayed in that awful marriage so long. I always thought, "Why didn't he leave?" Why didn't the counselors, after so many attempts, not counsel me to take my "biblical out" of adultery and go?

The choice to stay was my own. The wounds to my soul from my childhood and up through my marriage ached to be healed and have someone, even if he was lying, follow through with their vow to love me. I had waited so long for my daughter to arrive that part of my dream of having a child did not include splitting up her time with me, so I unfairly stayed longer to avoid that experience.

God has not changed his mind about marriage or divorce. He allowed stiff-necked people to extract themselves from an unfaithful marriage, especially when at least one of the parties is not repentant. My Jesus gave me peace that I had genuinely tried to work on and save my marriage. In the end, I had lost all respect for my husband, and trying to salvage our relationship was hard. But I was truly praying for a miracle and for my marriage to be saved.

On April 22, 2017, the divorce decree was final. I do not believe that God approves of divorce or has changed his mind in that regard. He does, however, allow it as an option when adultery has been committed. For twenty-eight years I was with this man; for fifteen years of infidelity I honored my vows and did not walk out on him. I went through multiple rounds of various marriage counselors, only to find out I was the only one trying. My Lord and my Savior honored me by setting me free, being my kinsman redeemer and providing a path forward.

When I told Ray to get out, I told him I forgave him because I could not carry that bitterness around with me. From that moment forward I tried to carry myself in a manner keeping with both my Christian faith and the example I wanted to set for my daughter. I did not bad-mouth him and in fact made him tell her what was happening, so she heard it from the horse's mouth.

She told me she had often turned down her television in her room, sat at the door, and overheard our counseling sessions. Some of which included the counselors yelling at me inches from my face telling me I needed to forgive him. Not a word about his repentance. She was devastated. When the separation started, she told me not to take him back if he asked because it was the most peaceful and joyful time in our home. She expressed that she felt lied to by all of us. My soul wounds were gaping and felt extremely raw for what I had allowed my baby girl to go through.

In my attempt to keep her from what was happening, I was withholding the truth, which is lying. All of this was mine to own. The Lord honored me by becoming my provider. The amount of time I spent on my face crying out to Him for peace and guidance was immeasurable. I thought the adultery was horrific enough. How my ex-husband chose to carry himself and treat me during the divorce thoroughly tried my ability to show him any grace.

With every turn, the Lord carried me through, allowing me to offer compromises and attempt to keep it all civil. At every turn, Ray refused to cooperate and dragged out this horrible proceeding. At one point, he even told me his goal was to drag it out and run me out of money. I did not recognize the man in front of me.

Finally, after a year and a half of chaos, mediation occurred. Whether we liked it or not, whatever happened on that day would be the law. It did not go totally as I had hoped, but for the most part went even better than any offer I made and therefore was my provision by my Jesus.

\* \* \*

Now the work on me would begin. While my ex-husband's adultery was the final straw for our marriage, I do not shirk responsibility for losing respect for him and seeing my marriage crumble for it. It also meant I needed work to become the woman God intended me to be before He would give my heart to any other man or that man's heart to me.

My entire life had been a line of men who were supposed to love me but did not. Some I inherited by birth. Others were of my choosing. All would become the training ground for my growth and spotlight where the wounds were and how the healing would begin.

Changes began in all areas of my life in preparation for my King. I required not one more thing to be happy, at peace, and definitely saved and in my Savior's hands. My Jesus was, however, going to walk me through the fires and high waters to show me what could be possible in the middle of His will and purpose for my life.

The spiritual portion of my preparations began with my ability to wade through conversations with other Christians regarding my divorce. The need for grace toward other believers who determined that if I had lost weight, wore more makeup, made myself "available" for my husband . . . and on and on, was the first trial. The assault this made on me and my senses left me speechless.

It was disheartening to me that everyone's first thought and remarks to me would be that I had done something wrong to make him cheat. If they only understood that this could have driven me from my church family and devastated me. My Jesus had prepared me through a lifetime of unrelenting abuse at the hands of others who were responsible. I chose to show them grace by not punching them in the throat but rather by walking away.

As believers, we tend to judge one another so harshly without knowing anything about what has transpired. I was not the only one who required discernment. Unfortunately, I am the only one the Lord was dealing with in my life at the time. He held my head above water, and I made it through.

The next dollop of grace was toward my baby girl. She struggled terribly with the divorce. On one hand, she was happy that the behavior was not in front of her any longer. On the other, she no longer had her family together. I chose to sit her down and apologize for believing I was doing right by her in keeping everything from her. I did not believe she needed the gory details, and I did not provide them at this point, either. I did, however, allow her to ask me questions, and if she asked ones that were the responsibility of her father to answer, I told her to engage him. This was one of the most healing times in our relationship and seemed to bring her a layer of peace. I cannot say we have not struggled, and we have our struggles to this day. But we are managing, and she encourages me that

I was and am a good example of a godly woman regarding any conversation about or treatment of her father.

The time for the hardest serving of grace had arrived, and it was for me. I do not think and have never thought I was perfect or even close to excellent regarding obedience. And most people may find it shocking to think that walking through the fire of my divorce was the worst time of testing in my life, considering all I had been through before that. I suppose it was because I made myself deal with and move on from each dose of abuse at the time it transpired and therefore my divorce was the trial of the day. My heart did not feel like it had any shards left to break. The devastation was total.

# Chapter 5

## For Richer, For Poorer

---

"True love isn't always romantic ... It's a choice to love each other for better or worse, richer or poorer, and in sickness or health."

–*Author Unknown*

---

When I met my future husband, I was a self-sufficient and successful woman. I did not NEED a man and therefore should have at least paused when some of the mental manipulation began. I truly cannot pinpoint the moment in time when I was not thinking about my own mental and emotional well-being. It would drive me crazy if my current journey had not taught me to let go of the need for this information, as it would change nothing now. Also, it would only cause me to be overly critical going forward, which is something I refuse to do. I want to get my mind right and allow any relationship with someone to unfold through interaction, not be questioning every word or action.

I entered my relationship with Ray on a purely physical level. We did not take the time to develop mental, emotional, and spiritual connections. If we had, there would, of course, have been a different tale to tell.

I had recently finished a semester at Mesa Community College in Arizona and taken a job working for a dear friend. My brother and sister-in-law had decided to have another child, and they would take back the caregiving of their children. Ray was working as an orderly at a hospital and was living at home with his mother.

While my work was challenging, I found myself drifting from routines that had been mentally enriching, like school-work and the voracious reading I had always had as a staple. The gym became more of the focus of my efforts as well as the initial glue that held our relationship together. It is ironic that a gym, in one form or another, would provide my boyfriend with enormous opportunities to stray.

At the time, there was not any internet or central location, like Google, to do my research on the science behind what I was doing and needed to do in the gym. I also wanted to under-stand how nutrition played a role in either losing body fat or gaining muscle. The trainer I had worked with had some good information; however, he was going off what worked well for him.

Ray had gotten a new job working for a professional body-builder who had founded a nutritional supplement company and appeared regularly on the radio. This gentleman would become a fountain of information for me, along with as many exercise, nutrition, and fitness magazines as I could get my hands on.

After moving in together, our routine became: work, gym, meal prep, and sleep. On the weekends, we went out with friends from the gym. I was not making time for personal growth other than in the physical realm. Atrophy in muscles that are not put to work is real. My brain was not getting a workout, and it started to show in a restlessness I felt.

The work I was doing was not breaking rocks, but it was not stimulating either. I decided to look around for something that could be my occupation and drive growth and creativity. I got a job in the nutrition industry which would be pivotal in many great career moves to come. I was not with this company long, but it lit a fire that drove me to pursue another position in the same industry, with the corporation called General Nutrition Centers (GNC).

Ray made the move to work with an agency with the state of Arizona that ran day programs for adults with developmental disabilities. They chose him for his size and strength as a bodybuilder for a specific client who was a rather large man and would require a firm hand. He enjoyed this work and became truly invested in the lives of the people he worked with.

My first position with GNC was as a manager at a small location in a strip mall in Phoenix that was floundering, as the area was starting to deteriorate economically. I loved the challenge and went in guns-blazing to start a revival. I garnered the attention of the regional manager and then those in the division. They came to me with an offer to manage one of the largest stores in southern California and be an assistant to the regional manager as well.

Ray agreed to the move if he could give notice to his current position and find job opportunities in California ahead of time.

He was also going to stay and finish our lease on our town-home in Scottsdale, so as not to bury us with the costs of breaking our lease.

I made the move to Costa Mesa, California, and through a friend I rented a room near work that would allow for month-to-month and to make the transition when Ray finally came out. When I went back to help pack up and ride back in the moving van, there were signs of an unhealthy attachment with a woman who had started working with him. He explained it away and claimed it was one-sided on her part and he could not stop someone from being interested in him. I was so caught up in the move and my new position that I accepted his justification.

\* \* \*

The move went smoothly, and Ray found a job by a recommendation of his last boss in Arizona. He was again helping adults with disabilities and was paired with another large man with autism and a smaller, older man who had had a brain injury when he was young. I discovered that GNC, especially in California, allowed businesses to employ individuals who are essentially wards of the state, to work part-time for a fair wage for their abilities.

So, I hired the two men Ray was working with, and they were the best employees I have ever had. If I gave them specific tasks, they did exactly what I asked and did not miss a beat. Seeing them three days a week was a blessing to both of us. They lit up with pride at feeling needed and accomplishing so much.

As with the store location in Arizona, I went about whipping this southern California GNC into shape with the same vigor. It had been one of their highest producing locations but had fallen in productivity due to their inability to find a stable manager. The store was located near a military base and a large retirement community, which were two of GNC's best demographics.

Once again, I garnered the attention of division management, and they promoted me to Division Inventory Manager. I had worked with my regional manager to develop an inventory swap which matched her store visit route. I got all the managers to speak with one another about shortages or overages of merchandise, and we would make the transfers of products from one store to another using the regional manager as transportation.

While working in the division headquarters, I progressed well, and they again asked me to take on training franchisees so those stores would operate in a "lean" fashion as well. This is when the desire to open my own franchise blossomed. Ray and I both wanted to go back to Arizona because of the high cost of everything in California.

We found our first location in a strip mall owned by Arizona State University in Tempe and began the process of making the move. We had both put some money away and were able to survive on our savings until our first store opened. For the first couple of months, we were our only employees, so we had to cover every shift. We would eventually go on to have four locations, two we owned outright and two we owned with partners that we eventually sold our interests to. I had my mother's entrepreneurial spirit, and this business challenge exponentially fed my mind.

\* \* \*

While Ray had extracurricular activities from the start, I believe some activity during our franchise ownership created a justification in his mind to accept from others what he thought he was not receiving from me. I was a voracious researcher and did not want to merely sell nutritional supplements. I wanted to help people on whatever journey they might be on. I believe he looked at running our GNC franchises as just a job.

At some point, when our employees would ask questions, Ray would respond, "I don't know, ask Michele." I did not think anything of it and did not realize how often it was happening, since I was not in the conversation when it happened. One Christmas, our employees had a baseball cap made for Ray with that exact response embroidered on it. It did not go over well. He laughed as he received the cap, and the employees laughed a little too hard, making him the target of their gentle ribbing. I was the one his resentment would be taken out on.

This was a wound for him that would not be healed during our marriage, and especially not by me. He had not had this as a justification for previous indiscretions but was taking advantage of it now. He did not have a relationship with Jesus yet and did not think his infidelity was a problem, since we were not yet married.

In my opinion, he felt disrespected, and he blamed me. He made the choice to work in our stores and either learn what was happening or simply have a job. I am wired to try to figure out the best way to do things or how to get the most out of the experience.

This is when he made the decision to get a job outside of our stores and became a personal trainer. Once again in the gym. One of his first clients would be the woman who would become instrumental in the demise of our marriage and hers.

\* \* \*

The mental manipulation that began, allocating the blame for his disrespect on me, would create a wound I suffered from throughout the remainder of our marriage. For a period after Ray did accept Christ, it seemed that he wanted our relationship to work. We agreed to "traditional" roles in our marriage, which developed a rhythm that seemed acceptable to both of us.

Shortly after the birth of our daughter, Ray partnered up with some folks who ran a specialty painting company, and this seemed to feed his creativity. This experience would eventually lead to the creation of our painting and cabinet-refinishing company, which still operates to this day. I was the one who studied for and took the tests to get the contractor's licensing, and while paint-contracting is not necessarily my wheelhouse, it was stimulating for me to be studying once again.

This new venture allowed me to be home for my daughter, and as she transitioned to school, I would start taking on more duties for the company. We would work home-improvement trade shows as our best marketing tool and then go out to give homeowners the estimates together for several weeks afterward. These always bore the best fruit for our company.

We got so busy that I was tasked with going out to formulate the estimates by myself, and I had a ninety percent closing rate. Our guys were some of the best specialty-finish painters and cabinet-refinishers in the state. Business was booming, and when Ray started needing to run errands even on Sundays, I did not question his comings and goings.

Control of my time and his money became a point at which we came to loggerheads. After the closing of our GNC businesses when both of us were working other jobs, my paycheck would go into "our" account, but the funds were always referred to as his money. Now that we both worked for our painting company, it was all his money.

Evidence in the form of receipts for hotel stays and the

sudden need for him to stay in hotels because a job was on the other side of town instigated his need to take over our finances and pay our bills. Marriage counseling with various individuals began. Every single one of the counselors was fascinated by what Ray did for a living and would spend a portion of our paid appointment talking to him about what he might do for their homes.

They loved him and determined that I was making a mountain out of a molehill. Needless to say, we would move on to the next recommendation for a counselor. My incredulity would go unnoticed and not one of them bothered to drill down as to what exactly was happening and why. Even in the presence of the evidence of infidelity, the counselors said I needed to forgive him and be grateful for a man who was working for his family.

My father all over again.

# Chapter 6

## Great Expectations

---

"I'm not in this world to live up to your expectations
and you're not in this world to live up to mine."

*–Bruce Lee*

---

It is difficult to think you are in your right mind after fighting a
lost cause for fifteen years. It is hard not to think you are stupid
when every time you answer the "why did you stay?" questions you do not have a satisfactory answer, even for yourself.
When you are sitting in a courtroom and after the judge asks
your almost-ex what he thinks you deserve after twenty years
of marriage and seventeen years of supporting his business . . .
he makes the first eye contact and says, "Nothing." You think
to yourself . . . *This is what I was fighting for? . . . This is what*

*all those years of being told you need to forgive him and believe he is doing right has gotten me?*

When I was young, I was fearless and bodacious and none of this crap would have gotten by me. None of it would have flown. Although I was not making great decisions by cutting everyone off before they could leave me either. Yet here I was believing and being told that I was doing the right thing by being forgiving and gracious.

It felt at least noncombative to have Ray agree to sit down and try to figure this out for ourselves without lawyers, at least for now. He agreed to let some friends of ours, a couple, mediate to lay out a peaceful divorce process. We did not get fifteen minutes into the conversation when he exploded and announced that it was his money, his business, and his house, and he was not going to give me anything.

Ray felt that allowing me to live in our house with our daughter and allowing me to ask for a small allowance should have been an overwhelming blessing to me. Any discussion on fairly dividing the proceeds of a twenty-eight-year relationship and a twenty-year marriage was off the table. He felt our friends were being one-sided because they thought me receiving something was fair.

So, without our friends, I made a couple more attempts to come to some agreement by ourselves. His only acceptable outcome was me receiving nothing. Even though he originally agreed to let me and Maya stay in the house, he even moved that position to selling it instead. I believe his true infidelity was with his business. It meant more to him than anything, and parting with any of his money or possessions was unacceptable to him.

My Jesus had me where he wanted me. On my face before him, humbled and asking for his will to be done. I had not asked this the entire time I had known Ray. The wounds of my own making were side-by-side with the ones ravaged by Ray.

Lawyers became involved. Everything Ray said or did from this point forward was rubbing salt into very raw wounds. He was unrecognizable to me. Trying to have a civil conversation and work out a settlement was never going to happen. After over a year of ugliness and lots of money spent on lawyers and other professionals, mediation was finally agreed upon.

No one gets everything they want in mediation. I did, however, get provided for by my King better than any one of the offers I had presented to Ray up to that point, and this gave me peace. Peace that I had not asked for anything unfair and that, as always, my Provider was there.

I made these choices myself and have no one to blame, but it did not change the feeling that my forgiveness and grace were completely manipulated and used against me. All of this made me feel as if I no longer had any critical thinking skills or ability to comprehend circumstances and make valid, truthful, fact-based decisions.

The fact is that none of what was going on around me was being viewed through the logic of any mental capacity. It was being viewed through the lens of the wounds to my heart and emotions, and this would be my first mistake. This would be my biggest mistake and the thing I most needed to correct mentally for the sake of future relationships and communication on any relationship level.

\* \* \*

Having expectations of any one human is a critical mistake. Logically, all of us will let each other down. Expectations set us up to let each other down, since they are rarely realistic. So, my task now was to find the ability to think logically about my relationships, not set anyone up against expectations, while allowing myself to emotionally connect as well. This cannot be done in my own strength and knowledge. Frankly, I do not believe any of us can . . . but this is my journey . . . and my reality.

I had to completely change my thinking. I think after the age of two, this becomes an impossible task! However, all things are truly possible with God. He tells us we have not because we ask not and that we ask outside of His will for us. So, it was time to ask, listen, and put the brain God gave me to work.

"The fear of the LORD is the beginning of wisdom, and the knowledge of the Holy One is insight." Proverbs 9:10, English Standard Version of the Holy Bible (ESV)

After my relationship with Jesus began, I started my "why?" journey. My mother told me I was born asking "why?" with insane curiosity about everything. I wanted to know how things worked and why they were the way they were. I asked my Creator about every aspect of His creation, and He kept showing me His word . . . and helped me follow the science.

So many times, I felt I was getting no answer as I kept asking "why?" The fact was that I had not fully incorporated all the knowledge He has already given us, and He needed me to calm down and catch up.

"Whoever can be trusted with very little can also be trusted with much," (Luke16:10a, NIV)

The Lord has given us much, and I was not even faithful with that yet, let alone in a position to ask for more. Not to mention, the amount of knowledge He has imparted in His word is enough for this lifetime on its own. Such rich guidance on relationships, communication, wisdom, and love.

\* \* \*

My marriage was over, and I had no visible means of support. During the separation, I had divine appointments with going back to school "pop up" in my social media feeds. They really do know what we are thinking. Years earlier, I had gotten scholarships to begin college and had only gotten enough credits for a little more than an associate degree. I felt this provision by the Lord had not been fulfilled, and it was time to complete my four-year college degree.

I had asked to do this during my marriage, but there was never the money for me, and Ray did not see the need, what with me already having my job working for the company. I prayed about it, and so many doors were opened. Even though my original college credits were earned a lifetime ago, Arizona Christian University reviewed everything, interviewed me, and accepted most of them.

Once again, some scholarship money was found, and I went back to school. I was in heaven! Classes, homework, learning, and through a faith worldview, there was nothing better than this for my mental healing.

One month after the divorce was final, I graduated Summa Cum Laude with my bachelor's degree in business administration from Arizona Christian University. My Peanut and close friends came to the ceremony, and she had a party waiting for me at home. I had finally honored the Lord's provision of access to learning and advancing my purpose, and there was no better balm for the wounds my father had left gaping.

I was enough. I was enough without him. I was enough in Christ.

# Chapter 7

## Broken Promises

"When you have sex with someone, your body makes
a promise, even if you don't."

*–Vanilla Sky*

The gym became the Urgent Care facility my body needed.
The wounds of a lifetime had not gotten any attention. I had
walked away from self-care and thought I was in control of
what was happening by distancing myself from anyone who
might love me after having offered myself to them. The abuse I
had suffered as a child had an impact on my physical chemistry,
and the choices I had made since then were not doing me any
favors either.

It is true that working out releases chemicals which are
better than any anti-depressant medication in the world. I un-

derstand how people can have a bit of an addiction to working out because of a genuine full-body "high" that drives your disposition for the remainder of the day.

The trainer called Vinny that my sister-in-law's brother introduced me to was a professional bodybuilder who had competed at the Night of Champions professional competition, so I felt in capable hands. He analyzed my diet and any exercise regimen which had been in my purview at any time in my life.

We ascertained quickly that I was actually not eating enough and I was drinking too much. He had me write down what I ate over a three-day period and asked that the time span include at least one weekend day. This was eye-opening for both of us and my introduction into truly focusing on nutrition.

Vinny wrote out what I needed to eat, and I was appalled. I absolutely did not believe I would do anything but get huge on his meal plan, and not in a good way. But my own preparations had betrayed me, so what did I have to lose? He jokingly wrote "Ms. Olympia" on my folder and told me he would have me competing as a bodybuilder by the time he was done. I informed him that he must be smoking a special kind of crack. Within the next year, I met my future husband who was a bodybuilding competitor and prepared for my first competition as well.

In the first month I worked out with Vinny, I lost twenty-five pounds and looked and felt better than I ever had. It was hard work, and I did not have a naturally fast metabolism. So, I had to get in there and work twice as hard. It was an absolute blast. My first bodybuilding competition did not go as planned but went well, nonetheless.

While I was preparing for this first competition, Ray made a date with a stripper. I was in the best shape of my life and never felt better about myself, physically, and yet he cheated. Every part of me felt that emotional scab get torn off.

So many people comment that a woman who has been through infidelity must not be in good physical shape or must not be doing certain things to be "available" for her man, when beautiful, in-shape women all over the world are regularly victims of infidelity. The world, and even members of the Christian community, want the woman to take the ownership of her man seeking another woman to satisfy his desires. Rarely will anyone speak about his accountability.

While living together before our marriage, we did not seek counseling for working out our exclusivity issues. We were in fact not married. However, it is the unspoken code that if you agree upon exclusivity and move in together, you are expected to be monogamous. Despite repeated infractions, I did not leave him. It very much had an impact on our physical relationship. We were "living in sin" out of wedlock and having sexual relations.

None of this excuses his behavior. I had not, however, consulted my Jesus, nor did I even want to acknowledge to Him my choices and activities during this time. This crazy cycle would go on for the eight years we lived together before the catastrophic decision to get married anyway.

\* \* \*

I remained in relatively good physical shape from this time through my marriage and ownership of our General Nutrition franchises. I became a certified nutritionist and felt better than I ever had about my body and actual health. At this time, some significant signs of another dalliance on Ray's part came to light. He did not appreciate being confronted and decided to move out.

We had to physically engage with one another while our fourth franchise was being remodeled, and we had to be there to manage the construction and the grand opening. It was incredibly stressful and wreaked havoc on my health. I wasn't eating much and therefore had unhealthy weight loss. Sleep was hard to come by as well. He had a way of making me feel crazy and as if nothing improper were going on.

In the middle of all the chaos of our businesses, we did come to an agreement to communicate and perhaps go on "dates." We went to a concert, and he invited me back to his new apartment to spend the night. Believing we were making progress, on the car ride home, I was hopeful. Upon arrival at his place, the air was let out of my balloon.

There was a gift bag hanging on his doorknob. I made him let me read the card, and it spoke of the incredible time the woman had had with him and how she could not wait to see him again. The gift was from a woman he'd met at a drive-through fast-food location we frequented. I was beside myself, and while using his bathroom to collect myself, I discovered a makeup bag which belonged to an entirely different woman. One who, I would later find out, was invited to our wedding.

Not a single wound from my childhood rejection was left unscathed by his behavior. I do not have an answer for how we got past this and got engaged and got married. The best explanation I have is that I believed for both Ray and my father . . . I was not enough. Who else would want me? This relationship was better than being alone. None of which had I discussed with my Jesus.

\* \* \*

I genuinely cannot recall the process by which we came back together. We got engaged shortly after he moved back in with me. We began a search to buy a home and were successful rather quickly. We set the wedding for one year from our move-in date to our new house to give us time to settle in and do the planning.

Physically, I did not feel right about the engagement and had no peace. I was thirty-three years old, and my hormones were all over the place, since we chose to get off birth control to be able to start a family right away. I was crying frequently and felt moved by the Holy Spirit to get back into a growing relationship with my Jesus.

Finding a church home and having a community of ladies took some of the weight of poor decisions off my shoulders. I could literally breathe better. While my little band of prayer warriors were lifting me up, Ray did not wish to attend church with me at this time, and I followed through on the wedding plans and was now unequally yoked.

Our miscommunication and lack of a joined faith world-view led to many disagreements and talk of getting married as a mistake. It appeared that we were going to have trouble conceiving, so we decided to investigate any infertility issues we might be having. My hormones were all over the place, and the stress in our relationship was not helpful.

Ray's decision to start attending church with me came out of left field but was a welcome revelation. Only a few months later he made his salvation decision, and this opened the floodgates for both my health and our hopes for having a family. I genuinely believe my Jesus now had us where He wanted us regarding our relationship with each other and with Him.

* * *

Six years after we opened our first franchise, the GNC corporate leaders decided to do some creative marketing that was catastrophic for several hundred of their franchisees. Most of the franchisees decided to file a class action lawsuit against the corporation. I was exhausted and did not feel I had the energy to see it through. We simply closed our stores' doors and made decisions about what to do next. As much as I wanted to have our stores for generations, the things that were about to happen gave me more joy.

I had been off birth control since well before the wedding because I was thirty-four and we decided we would like to start a family soon. We were three years into our marriage and were not having success getting pregnant, so we decided to take some basic steps to see if either of us might have any signs of infertility.

My cycle was like clockwork, so my doctor did not think I was having any issues. Because of Ray's steroid use, they thought testing him would be the best place to start. His first sample had blood in it from a back injury he had sustained shortly beforehand, so they requested another.

The stress of closing the business was taking a toll on my health, and I thought I was merely feeling sick from the anxiety. Having some symptoms of a sinus infection, I went to my doctor to see if they could extract whatever was trying to hammer its way out of my skull. They gave me a pregnancy test to be on the safe side before administering meds, as I did in fact have a sinus infection.

My doctors' lips were moving, and then she hugged me. I could hardly believe it and began to ugly cry because I had doubted my Abba Father was going to allow me to be a momma. Not because He did not love me, but because I felt I deserved that particular consequence. For me, a birth has never been more anticipated, with the exception of my Savior.

\* \* \*

The physical wounds I had endured had only appeared to heal. There were no visible bruises. No one had ever taken a look to see how my body had weathered those particular storms. Definitely no hormone or lab tests were done to see what my levels were or if I had deficiencies. I was thirty-seven, going to be thirty-eight by the time my baby was born.

To my chagrin, they treated me as if I were geriatric, attempting to send me to "specialists" who had experience with having babies at a "mature" age. My doctor was awesome because she had had her daughter around my same age, and she intervened in any demands my insurance company attempted to put on the situation. People were acting like I was Sarah from the Old Testament and my dusty old barren womb had been revived. I was only thirty-eight, for Pete's sake.

It is customary practice to give "mature" pregnancies a test called amniocentesis. The doctor uses a large needle to extract some amniotic fluid surrounding the baby in the womb. They explained that this would be able to tell me if there were any problems or genetic defects so I could decide what I wanted to do with the "fetus."

I had heard horror stories from mothers about how wrong these tests had been about their babies, as well as learned of statistics on how many times the test actually caused miscarriage. I told them I did not want the test, and you would've thought their heads would explode. "What if your baby has defects because you are old?" I informed them that, as a Christian, the only thing I was going to "do about my baby" was allow God's timing on her gestation and condition.

I was preparing to compete in bodybuilding again when I found out I was pregnant with my daughter, so I was in relatively good shape. I was nauseated for the first six months and lost eleven pounds. After that, I felt reborn and made up for lost time. My pregnancy was uneventful and like clockwork.

A month before the birth, they did an ultrasound, took measurements, and said she would be ten pounds. All I could think was that was the weight of my ball when I was on a bowling team in high school in Michigan. They asked if I wanted to pick the date and induce labor. I said I would prefer God's timing on when she was ready.

I had planned to go back to work after my family leave, but that all changed when I looked into my Peanut's big brown eyes. She was perfect. My beautiful little angel, sent from heaven. My Abba Father knew she would need me, but even more, my wounded little heart and soul would need her.

\* \* \*

At two months old, Maya showed signs of the eczema her father had experienced as a child. This would not only require an overhaul of her diet, but mine as well because I was nursing her. We also had to change everything in her physical environment. I did so much research that I practically had a PhD in every detail of eczema origins and treatments.

All of this meant that I officially would stay home with her, since any daycare situation would have to have extremely specific protocols for her to survive contact with any allergens. She was too little to narrow down what might merely make her itch and what might be deadly. I believe the need for my attention to my daughter's situation was further justification for Ray to find what he wanted outside of our marriage.

I did not lose the baby weight right away, and this added fuel to the fire when conversations about the other women would come up. One of his training clients was going to compete in a bodybuilding show and had asked him to go with her. The competition was out of town, and there would be an overnight stay. He told me he was going, instead of asking. When I told him that either he took me and our daughter or he did not go, he used a tactic that would become standard for him; he told me I was jealous because I was fat and his client was in the physical condition I only wished I had.

This was not a wound reopening, this was a fresh one, of his making. One that would fester for the remainder of our marriage. Sitting there crying, holding our two-month-old child, I stood my ground, and he gave in and did not go. It did not, however, stop his interactions with her or any of the other women, as I would find out later.

I took to heart his words, just as I had my father's, and I became obsessed with researching how to make physical changes in my body to prove him wrong. Not because I was jealous or because I thought the only reason he was cheating was because of my physical condition. But purely for me. To know I could and in doing so reveal that this was not his genuine excuse for treating me this way.

I decided to modify what I knew from my bodybuilding diets and did my own version of the Atkins diet. It worked well, and I got the rest of the baby weight off. Fortunately, I did this to feel better about myself and, of course, to remain appealing to my husband. Sadly, his adulterous activities and the affair which ended our marriage began around this time anyway.

Ray was never one to hold his tongue when I was looking bad and always managed to downplay when I was looking better. It was hard for me to take, and in hindsight I can see that he had no skin in the game for me at that point. It was about controlling me, my time, and any money I managed, and he would do as he pleased with his "side hustle."

\* \* \*

I rode a roller-coaster in weight for the next fifteen years and did things like the Atkins diet, HCG, and food group elimination. Some things worked dramatically. The HCG diet was crazy-good, and many people followed my lead and used my same professionals to do it as well. It is, however, extremely hard to move to any kind of normal lifestyle afterward, which made life challenging.

I have been told that women can begin menopause within thirty years of the time they first start their menstrual cycle. I began at menstruating at age nine. Doctors suspect this was the case because of the molestation I endured. On my initiation alone, Ray and I somehow managed to have a physical relationship enough for me to get pregnant again.

I was forty and had control of my own schedule to some degree. At five months, I began to have some abnormal cramping. It was the beginning of my miscarriage, and it took a couple of days. The pain was excruciating, and there was nothing we could do. My Peanut was two years old and would come check on "Mommy" and lay her head on my tummy.

Physically, when you have a miscarriage, you need to make sure everything comes out. Not only the baby, but the placenta as well. If anything remains in the uterus, it could be lethal for the mother. Doctors also generally do something called a D&C, which is scraping the inside of the uterus, to make sure the mother is safe. Due to my staying at home through my miscarriage, I was asked to bring any tissue I passed to my doctor. This meant the baby as well.

I had felt the baby coming out and made it to the commode. I now had to reach into the bloody water in the toilet bowl and get my tiny dead baby to take to the hospital for testing to make sure everything had come out. I lay on the bathroom floor with sounds coming out of me that I did not know existed. Ray was genuinely devastated as well and a little freaked out, as he had never seen me like this.

It crept into my mind that this was the consequence of what I had done. Having to see what happens in a miscarriage as well as a birth. Not because my Jesus did this to me, but because my body was responding to everything I had been through. One in four women have a miscarriage, so it was not really a "me" thing. But it sure felt like it at the time.

\* \* \*

In the middle of our marriage rollercoaster, I once again got pregnant. The physical anxiety was tremendous. I was on heightened alert over every twinge or pain. They say this would not be the reason I would miscarry, but our bodies react to the mental and emotional stresses we place on it, so I believe it at least contributed.

Four months into this pregnancy, all my fears came to fruition. Knowing what was happening did not make it easier. I was devastated. My little four-year-old Peanut came to check on Mommy again and laid her head on my tummy. She said in her sweet little voice, "Mommy, I'm not going to have a baby brother or sister, am I?" I wept uncontrollably.

She crawled up on the bed to hold me, and I explained that she would get all of Mommy's love and attention. She took my face in her hands, kissed my forehead, and said, "I love you, Mommy, and you can have all my love and attention, too."

I can confess that due to the lack of "love and attention" from my spouse, I allowed my daughter to fill the empty space in my heart. I do not know the exact impact this had on my marriage, as I believed he had left me already, at least physically and emotionally. This would continue the counseling journey for us and bring my Peanut—an innocent bystander—along for the emotional ride, to my dismay.

# Chapter 8

## For Better or For Worse

---

"Take each other for better or for worse,
but not for granted".

*–Author Unknown*

---

How long is too long? How many times do we forgive with no believable, trustworthy behavior being exhibited? Fifteen years was too long. God had not changed his mind about divorce. He had given us permission to leave due to infidelity, which was emotional abuse.

I thought making the decision to tell Ray to leave and finally end the crazy cycle was the worst pain I could physically carry. All the wounds of rejection by people who were supposed to love me were not only laid bare but cut deeper and several added anew. I did not want to reject anyone I had loved, as others had rejected me my entire life. The divorce process was worse than even what I had watched my parents go through.

Initially, I was exhausted and could not get a good night's sleep and felt the need for a nap regularly during the day. As much as his snoring had driven me crazy, the silence and the lack of a presence on the other side of the bed was unsettling. Peanut was fifteen, and I wanted to keep the semblance of a routine so we could find our bearings.

She was almost done with high school, and I had decided to go back to college to finish my degree, and we had to navigate time for her to spend with Ray. Maya was not happy about this part of her schedule. I tried to explain that she would not want to go on in life without a relationship with her father. She tolerated me and did not explain until later that she just wanted time to process all that was going on and not to be forced to deal with how she felt about him yet.

Through documents written up by his lawyer, Ray accused me of withholding her from him. This action made the court order a session with a psychologist for Peanut to determine what she really was feeling and if I was inhibiting her from visitation time with him. My baby girl cried all the way to the appointment and disclosed after the divorce was final that this was a pivotal point in some very real physical and health struggles for her.

Of the top of the list of anxiety-inducing circumstances you can go through, I had half a dozen on my plate. Anxiety is the most toxic thing you can do to your body, and it impacts every other area of your life. My body was reacting accordingly. It felt like I was living in *The Twilight Zone*. Some people I knew seemed to understand what was going on but reacted as if they were at a funeral and did not know what to say to me, so they said nothing.

It felt isolating at first, and I suppose that is exactly what my Jesus wanted for me. Time to work on me and how my life would look going forward. Despite the chaos which popped up daily with whatever new strategy Ray and his lawyer concocted, I developed a routine with the Holy Spirit to press into that relationship and reduce anxiety. This at least kept me from gaining weight and having mood swings, since I was entering menopause during this time as well.

* * *

While the physical presence of my ex was removed, my body had "phantom" pain from the rejection which kept rearing its ugly head. I was not leaning into what was true or real. I would look in the mirror and agree with Ray that no one would want that reflection. I saw the eleven-year-old little girl who was told she would not amount to anything without . . . whoever was delivering the line at the time. And on many occasions, it was me.

I cannot remember a time when I was not my harshest critic. Looking back on my life and at any pictures throughout the years, I sometimes wish I were as "fat" as I thought I was then. Truth is, I have never eaten a lot of junk. In fact, I am generally an emotional "non-eater," which might produce weight loss, but not necessarily the fat I would have liked.

I was not sleeping well and with my homework load, I was not getting any exercise outside of walking with a friend. I cannot imagine how wildly out of control my body would have gotten if I weren't at least doing that. I had learned what under-eating could do to my body from back in my early body-building days. I was on a budget waiting for the divorce to be settled and to find a job post-graduation. This allowed me to focus on eating at home, which helped control how food-preparation was handled. Making all my own food allowed for relief from the inflammation which my body was managing from all the anxiety I was experiencing from without and within.

The stress of the divorce was causing me to clench my jaw in my sleep. I would wake up with incredible tenderness all over my face. I could see the shift in my teeth, which up to that point had not had any issues. I went to Peanut's orthodontist and had them take a look. The decision was made to get braces to avoid any further dental issues and the potential for TMJ trauma.

Now my reflection showed braces on my teeth when I smiled or opened my mouth. There is nothing wrong with adults wearing braces. For me, it was an outward sign of the trauma my body was going through and a reminder of what I had been through before as a child. I was the little girl who had clenched her teeth to bear the burden of the wounds. Nevertheless, here we were, and I was going to be obedient to what was required of me to rectify at least the anxiety my jaw was channeling.

\* \* \*

The 2017-2018 school year would be Peanut's senior year of high school. It was also an incredibly emotional and chaotic year for every area of my life, which would set many good and bad things into motion for me physically. The divorce was finally mediated, and I thought that would lower my anxiety and allow me to attend to my emotional wounds, especially the very raw ones from the two years of the process.

Now, having to share parenting time with my daughter and navigate the events which come along with high school graduation, I had to press into my relationship with Jesus to control the impact on my health. Several people in my universe decided that I needed to know about Ray getting remarried. I had purposely blocked his girlfriend from trolling my social media because of my lack of control over my physical stress. She tried to "friend" me and Peanut, for what specific reason I do not know.

One friend in particular thought sending me a screenshot of their wedding photos was a good idea. I did not want Ray back and was not lamenting our divorce. It was the lies of fifteen years being published for all to see. One friend asked me, "Don't you think that's a little soon for him to be getting married?" Being a smart alec, I quipped, "Not really; they've been dating for fifteen years."

Several months later was my precious Peanut's high school graduation. We had a blast with her senior photo shoot, and the pictures turned out amazing. The process made her feel beautiful and gave her a semblance of control. We had to navigate who would come to a play she was in about a month before graduation as well as graduation itself. I was throwing her a party at the house and needed to brace myself for extending grace and inviting all of her family.

Ultimately her request was that all of her family on her dad's side would, of course, be invited; however, she did not want his new wife to be there. Ray honored her request, and several members of his family came to the graduation and several more to the party. This was the first time since the divorce, and frankly the separation, that I had been in the room with everyone. My whole family was there as well.

It was awkward, but Peanut was a good hostess, and we greeted our guests and made everyone feel welcome. I ached physically because our gathering had to feel this way. My home had been, and I hoped always would be, a place offering hospitality. While I am glad the Lord gave me the grace to extend to our visitors, it was hard on me that it had to be somewhat manufactured.

My graduation gift to my baby girl was a trip with our church to Greece and Israel. It was awesome and life-changing. Peanut told me regularly how, even though it might not show outwardly all the time, she understood what this specific trip meant and how much it cost, and she wanted me to know she was grateful. For two weeks, we escaped our world back home in Arizona and immersed ourselves in the land where King Jesus walked.

\* \* \*

Three months later, on the day before my birthday, I got the call. It was my mother's partner and the police, she was gone. I am not sure you could call what happened "crying." I was gasping for air and fighting for every move. It was as if I had had some type of stroke and multiple physical and emotional functions of my body were now going haywire or not working at all.

She had not been in good health, and we knew we did not have long. But many things about the circumstances of my mother's passing were not right, and I would never get answers. The medical examiner suggested she had been gone for a couple of days when her body was discovered. The police indicated that someone with senior services had come by to check on her, and even though her air conditioning was out in the middle of August in Arizona, no one filed a report or reached out to any of her family members.

My body bore the brunt of this. Under stress, I am a non-eater, and I lost twelve pounds in the two weeks following her passing. I was not sleeping well, and having to attend to my mother's trailer and belongings took a massive toll on my body.

My two brothers bore the bulk of the responsibility of cleaning out her home and helping collect anything that might mean something to the family. I am not sure I understand why we think a collection of things sums up a person's life. My little momma touched everyone she encountered. She was a firecracker and hard as nails, while being everyone's safe place to land. She genuinely loved everyone.

As a family, we took her ashes to Hawaii to spread on the ocean. It was a bonding time for us all. When I got back from the trip, I had a renewed sense of purpose to press into my Jesus and continue healing . . . everywhere.

# THE SOUND OF HEALING

## Beauty for Ashes

---

"He gives beauty for ashes. Strength for fear. Gladness for mourning. Peace for despair ..."

*—Crystal Lewis*

---

I needed to have my emotional and social head right for this process or I would not be any better prepared for a new mate than I was for my last one. While my ex's adultery is on him, as I came to realize that he was not going to get rid of the other woman during our marriage, I was not the biblical portrait of a wife, either. I had no respect left for him. I became someone I did not recognize, and that is not the example I wanted for my daughter.

So, now I needed to work out what happened to my twenty-year-old bodacious self who would never have let this happen for so long and my older self for not truly listening to my King as to how to best handle it all.

Now I was right where my King needed me. Broken and ready to see what He truly meant for me to become. In the middle of this process, my baby girl came to me and told me that while she could not understand why I wasn't "more mad at her dad," she saw how I was behaving regarding her dad, and everyone else who had an opinion about my divorce, and it was inspiring and an incredible example to her.

At this point, the only thing that mattered to me was my obedience to my King and that my daughter understood how a godly woman was to conduct herself. I felt I had let her down galactically as to how a woman should let herself be treated and how she should react to this treatment. To think that my obedience and preparations were getting through to her was an unspeakable unspeakable gift.

\* \* \*

During the divorce, all my relationships began to change. I did not post to social media or speak in public spaces my genuine thoughts about Ray or the divorce. To any friends who asked, I did explain what had happened. Those who were closest to me already had been witness to all the counseling and turmoil. Coming and going to church, people seemed to get an expression that said, *I don't know what to say, so I won't say anything at all.*

I got tired of my divorce being the only subject on anyone's mind. Sadly, it then appeared that there was nothing else to say to me. The invitations to dinner parties, which were mostly for couples, stopped arriving. For a while, I was included in invitations to social gatherings of either my small group at church or my women's Bible study.

For Peanut's graduation present, I took her on a trip to Greece and Israel with our church. It was awesome and life-changing for both of us. Up until Maya's graduation, we had been at the church and school every day for all her years of schooling. Now we would only be there for church services on Sundays and Bible study attendance on Wednesdays.

It felt as if the only reason I had been included in any functions for our small group and those friends from church was because I was married. I needed my church family, and very few of them showed up for me and Maya. This was a different type of wound. We are to love our neighbors as ourselves, and this starts with our church family. This felt like a rejection when I needed comfort the most. The aloneness became magnified.

On August 7th, 2018, I received a call at four a.m. to inform me that my mother was gone.

She had many health issues, and we knew we probably didn't have a lot of time left with her, but this was not expected and had nefarious undertones. I did not handle this well. My last conversation with her had been about her cancelling an outing where I was planning to take her to her doctor's appointment and lunch afterward. How my heart ached to have that opportunity back. My birthday is August 8th, and it cannot pass without me remembering my momma leaving us too soon.

\* \* \*

Another layer of loneliness created a malaise in me. I lost weight, but not because I was trying this time. One of the most important humans, who actually loved me, was gone. My Peanut was attentive and knew what losing her gramma meant. Since the divorce, I did not want Maya to feel like she needed to worry about me or be my companion. We did love doing things together, and we also traveled well together. However, I wanted her to spread her wings and not feel that she had to fill voids in my life for me.

My daughter was so gracious and compassionate and expressed her desire to see me find someone who would love me and not treat me poorly. She told me she thought I should investigate dating in whatever form that took, and she wanted me to know she would be okay with that. I would want her approval on whoever might make it through to be the man God had for me.

Maya and I cut a deal that by the beginning of the new year, if I had done the emotional work I needed, I would go on dating apps or put myself in situations where I could meet men.

I had spoken with a lot of people about their post-divorce relationship experiences, and their stories were as wild and varied as hotel choices in Vegas. Age plays a very real part in any understanding of where one goes to meet people. However, across the board, it all has the same cross-section of contestants. To play the dating game, men and women must compartmentalize their entire life into six to eight profile pictures, a 200-word bio, and some little quips which are supposed to be ice-breakers.

You may think I am only talking about dating apps, but when you think about even your friends trying to connect you with someone, this is the long and short of what each of you get before making the decision to go on a blind date. Every bit of this is terrifying for all involved.

Everyone complains that dating apps all suck; women use filters and lie, and men use their high school sports photos and lie. There is definitely a lot of that. But you also overhear or engage in conversations where you hear both men and women say how incredibly hard it is to find a date, let alone a potential mate.

Naively I thought, *I've dated before, how hard could this be?* I mean after twenty-eight years, had things changed? As they say in the comics, "What a maroon!" I was thrown into the deep end and was about to learn what I was and was not prepared for or healed from, the hard way.

I do not, nor will I ever, hold the sins of the men throughout my life against those to come. We all sin. We are all one choice away from being any one of them. I have been extended unimaginable grace, and therefore I am compelled to extend the same grace to other people. I was now going to step out and engage with men I was not related to and see if I could feel like a woman, like a daughter of the King.

* * *

I did not ask anyone I knew any questions about how to meet someone suitable. I simply saw ads and listened to some people talk about how they met their mate on this site or that. So, I dated in my twenties; I had this, right? As I write this, I am nearly crying because I am laughing so hard. Naïve does not begin to describe how much I did not know about the "dating app" process. Or, frankly, about dating at all. Unless you want to bar-hop and go to happy hours, you have to figure out how to intersect with men in your age group with your interests. This is tricky business.

I do not have any answers. I am here to tell you that we each must figure our own way here and not judge one another for anything. The rude comments and judgement I have received are indescribable. The people delivering them probably have good intentions, or not, but the result of their remarks crushing you and your spirit regarding your very personal decisions about dating are the same.

Dating is a very personal decision. It is between you and God what is to be your process. Yes, I eventually asked friends for advice and opinions, but the decision is still yours and you cannot allow what you genuinely want to be overridden. I had spent the last twenty-plus years allowing the opinions of others to dictate how I lived my life, and that had made me miserable. No more.

I chose a couple dating apps I had researched and took the leap of faith. The first thing you must learn is that truth is fluid on these sites. Even the Christian sites. The reality is that you are not going to meet someone online and get married without ever meeting multiple times in person and really getting to know one another. Even if I met someone sitting in the aisle in front of me at church. You still need to get to know one another and see if there is a connection and if each of you genuinely has a growing relationship with Jesus.

I am told I look younger than my actual age. My true age does, however, show up on all the dating apps as accurate. My initial experience with the apps was of having men much, much younger than me approach me first. No one in the five–ten-year age group either side of my actual age ever approached me initially. It was a crazy thing for me.

It was, however, a fun process and taught me a lot about what I was looking for in a potential partner. I went on many dates, and they all reminded me that there had to be the rebound guy so I could get my head together for my forever guy. It was nice to go to a pleasant dinner and talk to a male I was not related to and not have to pick up the check.

A friend had recommended a book to me by Dr. Henry Cloud, *How to Get a Date Worth Keeping*. Generally speaking, I believe his target audience was younger people who had not been married yet. However, he does speak to those who have been divorced as well. He talks about "getting up your numbers." Going on dates as an experience to solidify what you want and perhaps learn some of what you don't. It was fascinating how this magnified my patterns.

One of the processes Dr. Cloud asks you to go through is laying down your list. Not ignoring your deal-breakers, but just examining what if you stopped expecting a lot of extremely specific things that were probably self-sabotaging and had not been working for you in the past. I genuinely do not have a "type" regarding physical appearance but clearly had one regarding who I was emotionally drawn toward.

I got into an exclusive relationship with someone much younger, and we both knew it would not be our forever situation or lead to marriage. This fling was nothing more than a very nice transition for both of us and taught me so much about what I needed to do to be truly prepared for finding my "forever" mate. I do not consider that relationship a mistake or a regret any part of it, especially when I knew it would have to end from the start.

As I write this, I am making more emotional adjustments and grieving the loss of this relationship which had a stronger connection than I had planned. I will be okay and move on, and I am looking forward to very soon beginning the process of finding my forever guy. It was all very eye-opening. I thought I knew what I wanted. I thought I understood what had gone wrong in my marriage. I thought . . . that was my first mistake.

When people are taught how to recognize counterfeit money, they are taught what the real deal is. There is no ability to teach every possible forgery of money. So, the best course of action is to know the truth. Know the real deal when you see it. Well, I needed to slow my roll and let the Lord show me what the real deal looked like. A truthful, loving man of God with integrity, compassion, an active relationship with our King, and yes, I could have physical attraction.

The difficult part of dating in the age of dating apps is that people start conforming to the process instead of standing their ground. It is easy to let yourself drift a little on the things you thought were deal-breakers. And believe me, you will get pressed and pushed to move away from your inner foundation. You will get ridiculed and judged. Both from the other app "contestants" and from those who have decided your process is wrong.

You must take up your position and know . . . know for a fact . . . where there is room for movement and where there is not. This needs to be rock-solid, and you need to have this down pat before you begin. If you do not . . . you will be moved.

I may never have had a good handle on what to look for in a godly Christian husband. At the time I met and dated my first husband, I did not consult my God and did not pray much about the process. Ray may have gotten saved at some point in our marriage, and that is a wonderful God thing. However, it was obvious that he was not God's will for my life, at least not the way I went about it. God was honoring me, my prayers and my choices, nonetheless.

Now I needed to get things in the right order. I am not perfect and should not be anyone's godly example. My Lord and Savior has that job covered. What I needed to do was consult both my Creator and His instruction manual for what a godly man and husband looks like, but first, what a godly woman and wife needed to look like.

I had to get my house in order before I started looking. I feel that the Lord walked me through so much and felt relatively confident as I began the dating journey. However, I may have jumped the gun in believing I was ready quite yet. As I stated, I do not regret my experiences of this past couple of years or the relationships I forged. I do need to take all of this and make some emotional course-corrections before beginning the search for my "forever" guy.

*　*　*

After ending my temporary relationship, I was given the assignment of being alone. Not totally alone, as I would "be still" and know He is with me. But off dating apps, not chatting with anyone male, alone. I fought this for a couple of months and went on a few dates. A couple were no-shows, a couple were psychos . . . I wish those were the "no-shows." God speaks to us in a language we understand. I am a smart alec, and subtlety is not lost on me. So, He decided to punch me in the throat. I finally deleted all dating apps, stopped all non-edifying conversations, and this turned out to apply to some friends, who while well-meaning, were more like Job's friends, often unhelpful and sometimes even hurtful. Literally . . . alone.

My heart was hurting so hard that crying became a daily thing. I missed the connections I made on dates, even if unhealthy, because even the wrong kind of attention felt better than none at all. Not because it had any forever potential, but because it filled the silence. Now was time to start the challenging work of finding out why I needed to be alone, what I needed to learn, and how to be content alone.

My trainer, friend, and pastor Phreddie said something profound at this time that has stuck with me and given me comfort and hope. He said, "Maybe He is asking you to be alone for the last time." So, like I am being asked to be alone and work on some stuff and maybe my forever guy is too and then we get to meet? This was so heart-healing for me.

Some plans I had for travel were cancelled due to fires in California, which put me in a particularly alone position. I decided to do a staycation here in Arizona and do a little work on me. It truly was a great time. It was good emotional and spiritual work on me, followed by my own "high five" with the Lord, followed by a test, followed by galactic failure.

The good news is that it taught me how to look for the test and ready myself. This, however, was not without pain. This particular test showed me that I was once again lied to, and because of my love and connection I had overlooked the infraction. A wound which had never been completely healed had the scab torn off slowly.

While this was a good journey for learning and growing, it was devastating for my already-shattered heart. I did not want to believe I had once again walked head long into rejection . . . lying . . . pain. At what point was I going to stop doing this to myself? I had to come to terms with the fact that while other people lying to me or manipulating me was on them, I was teaching them how to treat me and what I would accept.

However, all of this was and is preparing me for what comes next.

The Lord answered me immediately and showed me that I was loving so hard and connecting so quickly and deeply that I was allowing myself to overlook predictive behavior which would lead to cheating, lying, abuse, and a lowering of my value. Sometimes the men I met employed manipulative and narcissistic tactics to continue the relationship and have the behavior go on and cement even deeper.

A couple of days later, I woke up at two a.m. and decided to ask, "How do I fix this?" Well, the Lord walked me through my significant relationships since birth, and it became clear that it was a mechanism I never had. I have, from my earthly father to this day, always found a way to excuse, forgive, and allow behavior for the sake of attention or connection. Always. Not a single relationship have I not walked head long into the wall of "abuse." "I" was not going to fix anything. That particular skill set had not been taken out of the box and for me had been broken since childhood.

Okay, so now what? How do I acquire the ability to not keep making these same poor choices without being cynical and looking for everyone I meet to fail? Well, the Lord is laughing hysterically at this point. I took a good look at all these relationships, and they had a lovely thread in common. I NEVER asked my Jesus about any of the men. Should I meet them? Should I go out with them? Should I stay going out with them? Should I marry them? So now I was going to fix this?

No earthly man has the wisdom of God. Solomon asked for it because he knew it was the most valuable thing. I cannot fix this. I do not have discernment or wisdom because I have not asked the Lord for it. I was broken . . . shattered, really . . . since an early age and never developed this skill set. I now needed to truly lay down my "right" to a mate or any relationship and allow my Creator to bring me healing and walk me into the right mind- and heart-set to deploy the wisdom and discernment, love, and compassion which He would bestow upon me, His beloved. This would then put me in the position to meet and truly see that the man God has for me is real and is ready for me, too.

\* \* \*

The Lord used so many methods to wrangle me. It was like herding cats. Direct revelation, scripture, and various authors who had travelled my road and spoken to my head and my heart. The ultimate reality is that until and unless I acknowledge the missing ability and also Who can remedy the situation, I will remain in the same leaky boat.

The book *Uninvited* by Lysa TerKeurst was very powerful

for me. At first, I thought it was going to be about something else regarding not being "invited" to things involving the circumstances around friendships. While this was part of it, it was more about the outright rejection involved in many emotional situations. This drove to the heart of the matter for me. And like Lysa, my emotional mess started with my dad and left a trail of broken pieces of my heart all the way to this day.

I had never developed the ability to truly see the big and small indicators that a relationship, platonic or romantic, might not be good for me going forward. Out of the pile of ashes of each time my life as I knew it burnt down, there was never a great "phoenix" with survival instinct revelation for me. I plowed ahead thinking my own special brand of "control" would be effective. I can not only hear God in my head laughing, but totally out loud.

Lysa spoke so totally to my heart through her own experiences and scripture that I thought someone had smuggled her a copy of my journals. I agree with her that when an author or speaker shares their deep struggles and victories, they have a much bigger impact than having someone preach at you or share stories from a perfect life which may have actually had some airbrushing.

I am not saying that someone who is truly dialed-in to their relationship with God cannot have a semi-perfect life or that they do not have anything to offer me. I have simply had the experience that in most cases there has not been the full truth, and that does not comfort someone who has been lied to and rejected their whole life.

I started out reading her book and marking impactful statements. I noticed I was highlighting entire pages and decided to just read. What I needed most was to come back to my "first love." Press into my relationship with God and realize that until I firmly held onto the love He has for me . . . I would keep grasping for . . . begging for . . . the "love" others showed me.

Rarely, well never, has the love I have been shown by the significant male relationships in my life been true. In every single case, I have been lied to, cheated on, rejected. Promises were made, I love yous exchanged, all "fake news." My heart so craved love . . . attention . . . affection . . . that I overlooked things that were obvious in hindsight but buried for me at the time.

I refused to be the one to reject loving and caring for someone, and this led me headlong into situations where I was used and taken for granted for that very same love and compassion. In all cases they expressed love for me and thought I was kind and compassionate. They then manipulated me to continue getting what they needed out of the relationship, without ever having to reciprocate. Now, their behavior was on them but allowing it . . . allowing it to continue . . . that, sadly, is on me.

I want more than anything to be genuinely loved . . . truly valued . . . truly in a relationship with a genuine connection in which I can share the rest of my life. And yet, here I sit accepting attention, affection, and love which is narcissistic and toxic for the sake of any attention at all. Again, I go back to not having developed the discernment to understand toxic behavior when I see it and to understand how truly loved by God I am and that I do not have to accept or beg for conditional, worldly attention from someone who does not have my best interests at heart.

As I finished reading *Uninvited*, as well as a couple of other books and scripture directed by divine intervention, I find myself deeply, genuinely asking for this discernment. I must warn you that just like the old saying about how when we ask *michele evette vrabel*

for patience the trying of our patience comes, ask for discernment of something specific and the test comes.

As my Lord had decided that subtlety was not working with me and more of a punch-in-the-throat style would be required, my tests came fast and furious each time I thought I had jumped a hurdle. I do not say this to complain. I found it comforting that I knew they would be coming. However, I cannot say I passed with flying colors. Some I passed, some I partially failed, some I failed galactically. Even in the failing, I felt good, as this was another opportunity to prepare for my King.

♡ 82

# Chapter 10

## Worse than Alone

---

"I used to think that the worst thing in life was to end up alone. It's not. The worst thing in life is to end up with people who make you feel alone."

–*Robin Williams*

---

To this day, I allow incredibly old wounds to have a stronghold on me which has created my current battleground. Making myself stay in the present with what is real and true is my struggle. The evil that has happened to me at the free will of others has me justifying irrational fears that somebody else's free will could hurt me now. The wounds are very real and very raw.

I pride myself in being a logical human being. Looking at the facts and the truth. However, the things which have so deeply wounded my heart will not travel the eighteen inches to my brain for a consultation. I genuinely believe my Jesus will provide for me or keep me safe. However, the choices of others have previously wounded me, and I have found no protection from their actions, which makes it hard for me to believe that in this world, those awful things could not happen again.

Let me be clear—I do not believe my Creator abused me or left me. It is by the Holy Spirit's guidance that my healing began, and I was shown how to survive all I have been through. But the fact remains that while I have a relationship with Jesus and rest in his provision and protection, the free will of other people persists.

The physical and verbal abuse which have left this fear in me have not happened, ever again. Yet their grip is very real. I have not had a break-in to my home since my childhood, but perhaps because the intruder was my father, and we did not see or hear his invasion of our sanctuary coming, the low-level terror of the thought of it haunts me. I realize this usurps my position of faith and trust in my King Jesus, and that is why it is a wound which desperately needed attention.

Along with my desire to understand why I was a target for men who choose to lie, cheat, and manipulate, I found myself in very real need of emotional awareness and the discernment not to let them thwart future relationships or stunt my emotional awareness.

Instead of trying to "break" old habits, where focusing on an issue causes it to be even harder not to "fall off the wagon," focus on and train for new behaviors. Telling a two-year-old, and even some fifty-year-olds, to stop something they are dead set on, never works and can end in a spanking and tears. Giving them a different toy or project gives them freedom of expression and a place for all that energy. We are the same. Only as adults, we don't think anyone has the right to tell us no. And we believe we have worked hard all our lives, so we get to make our own choices.

♡ 84

Is it healthy to have a feeling from an old wound come to mind? Is there anything wrong with remembering something which made you feel good? It is impossible to stop memories or feelings from cropping up when something prompts them. The Holy Spirit showed me that the best way to work with the system is to allow myself to feel them. Enjoy the memory, allow the oxytocin to release, and then welcome yourself back to the reality that that situation is no longer your current reality. Not that you come sit in some sad rabbit hole of aloneness, but that you realize where genuine love and appropriate attention exist is in the presence of God.

He showed me that our feelings were created as part of us as well and that allowing happiness and joy to flood over us within a memory is incredible. If you cannot stop a painful memory from showing up, embrace it and allow yourself to release it on your own terms. Use this technique to develop discernment to look for those good things in relationships going forward and know how to see the truth in both those and the memories you do not wish to repeat.

Focusing on and battling in the attempt to stop feelings or memories from resurfacing only causes anxiety in the waiting for it to happen. What a beautiful release of anxiety it is to know we can "feel" without dwelling anywhere that is unhealthy or where we do not wish to be.

\* \* \*

Not making excuses—only revelation of reasons—when I look back at all the relationships I have had where emotional abuse was a component, I cannot help but think, *What part did I play?* Clearly, each and every one felt some justification in doing what they did. Doing it to me specifically. Yes, they did to others as well, but for me, why did they believe it was

85 ♡

acceptable and why to this day do they justify their actions and not take ownership of what it really was?

Early on in my divorce, it would incite a low-level rage in me when someone would make comments about what I may have done to drive Ray to this behavior. The reality was that he was like this before I got to him and did not change throughout our relationship. I have come to understand that when someone makes choices to lie, manipulate, and be unfaithful, they know how to choose a partner who will let them get away with that as well.

I do not believe there is some character trait of mine which was the excuse for the bad behavior of the men in my life, although that is what they say. My brokenness and vulnerability made me easy to manipulate and feel shame, so forgiving them and allowing these behaviors to continue would develop a kind of routine for them.

Not for one second do I believe I am perfect and have no stake in how every relationship I have had has developed and turned out. I did not consult my Jesus or press into my relationship with Him until I was neck-deep battling for another man not to reject me.

Each of my relationships, platonic and romantic, have had beginnings which did not necessarily involve a consultation with my King. To that end, I cannot lay at the feet of others the blame for the relationships disintegrating when I finally woke up to the wreckage. I genuinely believe that to have friends and to have romantic relationships, we need to be where God wants us also. These relationships are important and should not be entered into lightly. Especially if they assume a place of access and counsel.

The Holy Spirit guided my "new" prayer to be about how to become the woman God intends me to be for the man or friends whom He has chosen for me. That would require looking in the mirror. That would require an examination of the old wounds and how the healing was coming along.

\* \* \*

On February 15, 2025, I deposited my final alimony check. I did not yet see what my total provision looked like, but my King Jesus has never left me. It did, however, bring up feelings that somehow Ray had been still in the mix until now. That I was not truly making it on my own. As with my father when I was eleven, I felt the trepidation that it was "just me" from here on out, while knowing that it has never been "just me." How would this look? Am I an imposter? Can I genuinely make it without any of the men who'd been a part of my life?

The revelation from the Holy Spirit that I had not been tending to that particular wound was breathtaking for me. I thought I was doing an excellent job of managing and disposing of how I felt about both my father and my ex-husband rejecting me and making me feel as if I were not enough. I felt I was doing good things and succeeding despite their predictions.

The fact is, I was. But internally, at heart level, I was using the measuring stick and was not going to go public with the data. It did not matter that what I believed about myself wasn't above the surface and on my face every day. It was there. How would I ever heal and allow another human to have that kind of access, that kind of input, if I did not clean out those old wounds and admit out loud what they were doing to me?

Self-isolating was made easy for me by the fact that so many people avoided me during and after my divorce. For the last five years, I can count on one hand those friends who were a part of my life while I was married who have reached out to see how I am or to get together.. At first it was painful and hurtful. Then it felt protective and as if I could control who could hurt me.

\* \* \*

The Covid-19 lockdowns provided the perfect justification to keep myself and my feelings behind closed doors. My emotional healing is an area where the wounds are still raw and are taking their time healing. This is not because the Holy Spirit has not been showing me the way. I have allowed the lies of horizontal voices—those here on Earth—to keep ringing in my ears.

Trying to buck against remembering, good and bad, has been a battlefield I created for myself. Then I cry out to get a little help here to know how to avoid the landmines. While healing is a process and we will not fully accomplish it this side of heaven, I have been given very real revelation as to how to tend to those particular wounds.

I have lived in my current home since 1995. I moved in with my future husband, and it was our home for the duration of our marriage. My daughter was born here. Our business, our church, our friends, and the experiences we had as a family are all within a twenty-mile radius. The likelihood that I will never have a memory of all those years pop up is infinitesimal.

When I was a little girl, we moved so much that there really is not anything from my childhood capable of sparking memories, and until I wrote my first memoir, *Butterfly Stitches*, I had not given them much thought. One of the first things I thought to do when the divorce was final was to go through the house and remove the "memories."

This was hard because most of them were in the form of pictures and a lot of them contained my daughter. I do not hate my ex. I have forgiven him because I cannot carry that. However, I did not want to see his face around every corner.

Funnily enough, after the pictures were removed, I discovered that the actual house did not hold many painful memories.

Perhaps because his infidelity was a road show. Don't get me wrong, there were arguments, and the rejections of my intimacy initiations were definitely shadows in the corners. But there were a lot of good memories in the house, and it was the only home my daughter had ever known, so fighting for and being awarded it in the divorce was a good thing.

This purge was a good first step. My daughter and I decided to take real steps to keep our new home peaceful and as drama-free as possible. I let her know she will always have a safe place to land and talk to me about anything, including about her dad. But we agreed that we were going to talk about moving forward and about solutions, not only about difficult situations.

We then set about making happy memories of our new life, the life I was now going to lead. My daughter and I do exceptionally well traveling and taking on adventures together. She got my interesting sense of humor, and it makes for incredible laughs while helping us learn more about how each other looks at life.

Now the more challenging task of the healing journey of all my other relationships, both past and future was about to begin. Even though forgiveness had been doled out, it does not mean that those wounds had even been looked at, let alone tended.

The Holy Spirit showed me I was being given the understanding to go forward knowing that, where pertinent, those wounds were caused by others and no fault of mine. On the other hand, the ones of my own making needed attention as well. I think my thought process was, "out of sight, out of mind." It does not work that way because until you accept and learn for the healing, the old wounds are always impacting our decisions.

Most counselors or professionals in the emotional health spaces want you to reach out to your broken relationships, if they are still alive, and enact some type of reconciliation. I am not saying that contacting people who traumatized me in the past is necessarily a terrible thing. I am saying that is not the process the Holy Spirit and I have agreed upon as my journey.

For me, those past relationships had contained lying and rejection which was not recanted, and therefore interacting with those people again would have meant re-opening old wounds. You can forgive and begin the healing process without another soul in the room besides you and the Holy Spirit. This is the process that my heart could handle.

\* \* \*

My heart healing began with me. Me finally praying about what relationships were "for me" and I "for them." Me releasing the ones which were not supposed to be there in the first place. Me accepting those which were only for a season. Me listening to my King Jesus about my identity and worth and how and where I was to look for the relationships He has for me.

When you are by yourself after a lifetime of never living alone, this is easier said than done, as a human anyway. Nothing is impossible with our Creator. When the loneliness is so quiet that it is deafening, you need to bring in your team and listen to those vertical voices only.

Since my divorce and the attempts at dating as well as trying to find my "tribe" in this new season, I allowed myself to partake in receiving attention for loneliness' sake and for the oxytocin release of attention at all. This put me in the position of needing to detox from those who had access and input to my heart. After a lifetime of rejection from those claiming to love me and being a "words of affirmation" gal, unhealthy attention with all the right words is a perfect storm for me putting my heart back on the line.

My Abba Father, my King Jesus, and the Holy Spirit and I meet every morning, and they lavish mercy and words of affirmation on me. They show me that while I am by myself, I am not alone and that their attention is the only, and the healthiest, attention I NEED. Would I like to have a man whom God alone has in mind for me? Absolutely. But what I NEED is to have a healthy understanding of what a relationship which God intends for me looks like.

One of my life-lesson Bible verses was now to be deployed. "Everyone should be quick to listen, slow to speak and slow to become angry" James 1:19 (NIV). Quick to listen has not been my strong suit. More like, while listening, I formulate my rebuttal. That is not how my King Jesus rolls. He does not hesitate to let me walk through the same testing over and over until I get the learning.

*\* \* \**

A sweet friend often got a word from the Lord for me. Sometimes I liked them, sometimes not so much. But every time they were exactly what I needed. I was married at the time, so this exercise had more to do with friendships, but now it applies to any future romantic relationship as well.

She told me to get a journal and begin making two lists. The first list had the traits I was looking for in a friend relationship. The second list was traits I brought to the table. AKA, the adage, if you want a friend, be a friend. If you want someone kind and trustworthy, be kind and trustworthy.

This exercise was not designed for me to hold up a measuring stick to others. It was designed to make me look at myself and see how I place unspoken expectations on others. It is very convicting to see it all in writing. Upon completion, I laid down my pen and talked with my King about the work I had to do to become who He had in mind for the relationships that would be suitable for me.

Time for a new list.

Again, not for imposing expectations or ruling out relationships with some version of newfound discernment. All this began cleaning out old wounds and allowed me to see how I was operating in my emotions. How I was teaching others how to treat me and accept toxic, unhealthy relationships for the sake of someone to love at all.

When I was shown the way out of the weeds, the journey got lonely, but the vision became clear. The unhealthy relationships I was in were not solely because of the others I was in relationship with, although they did play their part. It was because I was operating from a wounded and raw position and that, my friends, can never lead to good emotional health.

Placing expectations on others, especially without communicating the expectations, is a recipe for next-level heartbreak. Including ourselves. My relationships had been conditional since birth. The only unconditional relationship I ever had was with my King Jesus. Understanding what genuine a relationship with another person is supposed to look like was my new training ground.

Every bit of who we are and what we have been through is the lens through which we look at everything. This is not bad or good. It just is. Understanding that everyone else has their own lens, too. Entering relationships should be about genuinely connecting with who the other person "is," not who we want each other to be.

I had not entered relationships thinking anyone would change for me. I love everyone and wanted to be friends. Not everyone wanted to be my friend. Instead of my heart understanding that all eight billion of us do not have to be friends was the lesson I needed to get through my head. The defense mechanisms I developed over a lifetime have made me "quirky," to say the least. I would quip, "I may not be everyone's cup of tea, but I am someone's gin and tonic," for laughs.

The fact of the matter is that I wanted to know what was wrong with me, if I wasn't someone's cup of tea. I did not want to drag anyone into being my friend, but it felt like the lifetime of rejection over and over when I would see a group I had been a part of socializing regularly outside of our group setting, and I was never invited.

Truth be told, I did not really feel like I fit anywhere as this particular healing journey began. I suppose that getting me by myself has been exactly what the Holy Spirit had in mind to give me a good look in the mirror and determine what kind of friend I actually am.

When I meet people, I get invested quickly. I give access to my heart quickly. This opens wounds and brings heartache from the rejection when my enthusiasm for a relationship isn't reciprocated. Since my divorce, the pendulum had swung the opposite way. I became cautious with access. I found myself seeing reasons the other person will reject me first, so I was not surprised if it happened.

This was not healthy either. The Holy Spirit has had me focusing on truth and reality. I do not know if men do this, but women are great at going down rabbit holes of "what if" scenarios which have no basis in reality. The poor soul who is the subject of this drama has no idea you have taken them on this journey.

A scripture that would become my mantra to all my healing, but exceptionally for my heart: "Finally, brothers and sisters, whatever is true, whatever is noble, whatever is right, whatever is pure, whatever is lovely, whatever is admirable—if anything is excellent or praiseworthy—think about such things." Philippians 4:8 (NIV) We cannot stop the emotions of past experiences coming to the surface when something in our present brings them up. We can, however, deal with them by acknowledging what is real and true and not letting them dictate how an hour, a day, or a life is going to go.

Meeting new people, going to a new church, joining like-minded groups, all created an anxiousness which impacted every area of my life. Not all necessarily bad. However, our hearts, minds, and bodies do not know the difference. Focusing on the anxiousness can only cause it to grow. The Holy Spirit showed me how to allow myself to "feel" and accept an emotion as it comes up and walk it out. Then release it and not allow it to rule my actions.

Good anxiousness for example, like that feeling on a first date, a first kiss, or an exciting vacation, is exhilarating. However, you don't want to stay on rev forever. Allowing this excitement to heighten your alertness can help you turn that energy to discernment and ultra-tuned-in hearing from the Holy Spirit about the relationship you are entering.

Overthinking is a major culprit in producing feelings of anxiousness, especially for women. Listening to the horizontal voices of other people telling you your anxiety is a lack of trust in Jesus. Don't get me wrong, it could be, but it isn't always and hearing that can amp up your anxiety even further.

What the Holy Spirit has taught me from every angle about how to deal with anxiety is that I cannot stop from feeling it altogether. I can pray about it and take an audit of what is real and what is true.

Choosing to hear from the Holy Spirit each morning before my day begins has been life-changing for me. Gaining wisdom and understanding to have the emotional intelligence to look at each and every experience through the lens of truth and reality provides a calm—a peace which passes all understanding and which I alone cannot manufacture.

It may sound simplistic, but that is the beauty of the presence of the Holy Spirit in our lives. One hundred percent of the power of the God of the Universe resides in us. It is more than enough. More than enough strength. More than enough courage. More than enough peace.

Talking with other people may seem helpful on the surface, and saying things out loud definitely can feel like at least a little of the burden is lifted. But the reality is that all it does is speak over you and create a thought loop and plays over and over.

Of all the weapons I have acquired which prepare me for emotional healing and for that specific battlefield, the Sword of the Spirit, the Word of God, has no equal. The more I abide and press into my relationship with the Holy Spirit, the louder I hear His voice. If you are not hearing Him, have you talked to Him AND spent time listening? Genuinely leaning in to hear what He has to say about what you are walking through?

Whether you are a believer or not, I want to introduce you to the Holy Spirit, my Abba Father, and my King Jesus. I want to show you what their healing journey for me looks like and how it can be the beginning for you as well.

My daily routine is my best defense for not letting any voice, including my own, dictate how my day will go, other than my King Jesus.

# Chapter 11

## Board Meeting

---

"For there are three that bear record in heaven, the
Father, the Word, and the Holy Ghost; and these
three are one."

*–1 John 5:7 (NIV)*

---

Never alone. Never forsaken. However, sometimes by myself
genuinely can feel that way. I did not consider my marriage
ending anyone's fault or look to cast blame. It was, however, a
hard wound to begin healing, since the reality was that this one
came from my own hands. How were my relationships, with
my King Jesus at the center, going to look going forward?

The Christian community, my church family, and all my
friends—believers or not—all had opinions about what I needed
to do or how I needed to act. There were a lot of "never" and

"always" statements thrown around. Most of which had no biblical basis and were more an outpouring of their opinions of what I had done wrong and how I should change.

During the divorce proceedings, and at least until Maya finished high school, we continued as members of the church which we had attended as a family. My Sunday morning Bible fellowship class finally settled into not asking for the details of the process and more into how they could pray for me. There were a couple of other women who were walking the same journey, and we all bore the same look of exhaustion at this being the only topic discussed with us.

The interaction with my church family was dwindling as my daughter graduated and I was no longer on the campus for anything other than Sunday services or Wednesday ladies' Bible study. The church had a change in leadership, which caused a shift in attendance. Several of the couples who had been at least church friends were now attending elsewhere, and our interactions dropped dramatically or altogether.

Social isolation was already creating further loneliness for me when the Covid pandemic hit and made the isolation semi-permanent. I don't know if it is because I had been on social media and people felt they knew how I was doing or what the thought process was, but no one felt the need to check on me or see how I was doing, merely as a friend, not as a divorcée.

This lack of contact made me feel disconnected with my church family, and as I prayed about it, I felt called to seek where my King Jesus would have me connect. It was disheartening that as I made this journey, no one reached out to ask why I was leaving. People who had been my church family for over ten years literally had nothing to say to me.

It felt like the church door closing in my face all over again, the way it had when my mother left my wildly abusive father. What had I done to deserve this rejection? The Holy Spirit gave me peace that this was in fact the decision for me. It did not, however, lessen the sting. Several of my church friends told me to check out their new church homes. Not because of their attendance, but because I felt the Holy Spirit showing me that my "alone" journey was to continue, I was not compelled to check out those other churches.

There were former members of my previous church at a couple of the churches I was led to, but they were large congregations, and so I did not have the feel of bringing those conversations along with me. During the Covid lockdowns, I watched a couple of different online services, and one in particular resonated with me. When the restrictions on public gatherings were lifted, I began to attend in person.

\* \* \*

During this time, I was praying about and making decisions regarding many relationships. I was figuring out how to maneuver dating, choosing the right church family for me, and how to genuinely hear the voice of God on the matter.

As I had told my daughter, you need to have your foundation before you find yourself in the middle of a date where you are being asked to cross a line you never established. Dating is interesting in the Christian community. It is a zoo at large, but is also amusing in the loopholes older, newly single Christians will find to justify some of their dating choices.

Mind you, I include myself in this focus group. My healing had begun, but some of the deepest wounds were taking their time, and this opened the door for a change in the color of the flags which would crop up when meeting someone who could become a dating relationship.

I had made my list of requirements, and on it one of the non-negotiables was that a potential romantic interest needed to have a growing and active relationship with Jesus. He had to be kind and treat other people well. As a Christian, he would not be looking to "hook up" but rather would be looking for a long-term relationship leading to marriage and then intimacy. He would have to be willing to attend church regularly with me.

Upon praying about my list and my "lines," I made my choices of dating apps and singles groups and took my first step. I was not remotely prepared for what I was about to see, hear and witness in the behavior of others, nor my reactions to all of it.

* * *

I posted my profile on several dating apps I researched, being extremely truthful, with the requisite pictures and short bio about who I am and what I am looking for in a potential date. Some of the preference options are a bit of a catch-all, so you cannot assume anything. For example, the "religion/faith" preference. If you select Christian, this could mean every religion that has a church building. The apps allow you to indicate on the preferences if they are deal-breakers and are supposed to sort out the options they show you accordingly.

I learned very quickly about the "tricks of the trade" for those who were looking to scam newly single divorcées with promises of long-term relationships, soulmate-seeking, and good "Christian" men. I would imagine the fellas have the same issues on their end. As I entered conversations with those of like-minded faith worldviews, it became apparent that sometimes their devotion to the Lord was only "bait" to get me into conversation.

This was not true of everyone, and I do not think every single person on dating apps is a "player" or a scammer. But there are a lot of them, and it makes the dating scene not as much fun as I remembered in my youth.

It became disheartening to begin conversations with reportedly Christian men who asked to come to my home in the second sentence of our chat. I understand the irony regarding my temporary romantic relationship at the beginning of my dating journey. But as I course-corrected and listened to the Holy Spirit on healing and on discernment, it became easy to see why in my broken, wounded condition, I felt like anyone who showed me attention was a good option.

I did not believe I needed a man to be happy or to have a blessed, joyful life. But it seemed like it would be nice to have a godly man who actually loved me for who I am. The issue with this—as the Holy Spirit showed me—was who exactly am I? If I had not healed and did not know who I was or understand what a genuinely godly man or relationship looked like, how was I any better-equipped to enter said relationship?

Perhaps anyone else would have been allowed to date while healing in order to learn. I am not that gal. I was not holding the line. I was willing to reopen the wounds to my soul out of the almost-desperate desire to have someone love me. This was not a good environment to start any relationship. Not even to acquire new friendships. The Holy Spirit needed me to abide in the only healthy relationship in my universe until He let me know it was time to step out.

\* \* \*

The Holy Spirit is not an "it." He is real. He is God. He is the Counselor and Comforter. He has and always will be part of the Trinity. He was Creation. He guides us and gives us the wisdom from before we were created to understand and reconcile what is going on. The moment we are born, we start working things out, using the critical thinking skills He gave us.

First, we discover that Mommy is the source of love and nourishment. Every single experience from there on is a teachable moment. Whether good or bad, every single experience teaches us how to act or react as we progress through this life. Usually when things go awry is when we allow our "feelings" to override what we know to be truth from the Holy Spirit.

While we receive the indwelling of the Holy Spirit at salvation, from the beginning of your life He was there all along. In the telling and hearing of your story, He shows you how you had the knowledge to make decisions and reason out what was going on, which would either help you heal or change your trajectory. The Holy Spirit does not just show up at Salvation. We have a relationship with Him from the beginning.

This relationship IS the healing. Seeking Him. Finding Him. Listening for His voice alone.

# Chapter 12

## I Shall Not Want

"David didn't always get what he wanted every day. But he never lacked what he needed any day of his life."

–Louie Giglio in *Don't Give the Enemy a Seat at Your Table*

The first steps in any healing or recovery always begin with you. My whole life, I had worked things out based on logic and kept asking the Lord for additional wisdom. He does tell us to ask. I have learned that He tends to speak to us in the manner which fits our personality best, and I am a smart alec and respond best to intelligent wit and humor.

So, to that end, He had been growing my wisdom by putting me in situations which required some. I kept asking . . . He kept sending the trial . . . I kept failing. I asked, *When did I lose my wisdom and discernment?* After bending over laughing, He reminded me I never had any to lose. It sounds trite and simple, but the reality is that I had spent an entire lifetime dodging the pain and therefore the lesson along with it. This was a huge revelation for me, and now was the time for me to pay attention and listen for the answers to exactly what I had been asking.

Years ago, I had gone through an incredible Kay Arthur Bible study program. It caused me to look at more. This was before the internet, so I had to do it the old-fashioned way; head to the Christian bookstore near me. I found several study guides and loved them all. One which has stuck with me all these years was on inductive Bible study.

Inductive Bible study is a method of studying the Bible which focuses on extracting meaning and insights directly from the text itself, rather than starting with pre-conceived ideas or external interpretations. It is a process of observation, interpretation, and application, leading to a deeper understanding of the text and its relevance to your journey.

I have since then purchased an Inductive Study Bible which has been my constant companion. I can "create" a Bible study anywhere, anytime, on any book where I feel led to do a deep dive.

Well, my King in all His humor led me to the Book of Proverbs, the wisdom book. This was the first Bible study after my divorce was final and would truly lead me to a space where the forgiveness I doled out to my ex really took root, my peace and joy start emerging, and real knowledge and wisdom were not only becoming clear to me but were finally sticking.

I had never developed the discernment to see and avoid the red flags which should have chased me off any relationships in which they cropped up. Because I had been abandoned and rejected as a child by those who were supposed to love me, I was not going to be the one who did the rejecting . . . period. Far from the logical premise in which I thought I was operating. I am an academic geek and genuinely love the deep dive of an inductive Bible study. The Book of Proverbs was the meat I needed, and the Lord had set the table well.

I have read the Bible through at least a dozen times in my life, and yet I always am shown something divine every time I break out into a specific book. Proverbs was no exception and truly lived up to its reputation.

I have sixty-six books of wisdom from my King and until I have managed those . . . I am not asking for outside wisdom so I can utilize what He has walked me through thus far. I love that it culminates in Chapter 31 with the Proverbs Woman. Some women find it daunting and asking too much. I find it the perfect bar to set. It is my own fault that I have allowed distractions and have lowered my own value, causing the Proverbs Woman to be anything but an incredible example of what is truly possible as God's creation.

Inductive Bible studies break things down by the five Ws and the H. Who, What, Where, When, Why, and How. For me this sets the best stage for context in every area. I know the time in history and how the culture would react to the message, so I can translate the application to contemporary times and myself. It does it in a way that simplifies the message as well and does not make you feel like you need a theologian to decipher the meaning.

I believe in gathering with my church family for services on whichever day the church meets. It is important to be there for one another and receive the teaching from your pastor and encourage others. As well as serve in some capacity, both in your local church and in your community as well.

I think small groups which meet during the week are an

even better community where you can make deeper connections and hear from others who are in a similar season of life or are walking a familiar journey. I participate in all of these. We are left here after salvation for the purposes of creating community with one another and leading others to Christ.

We also need our own, intimate, personal time with our King to understand His perfect will and purpose for our lives. This is where inductive Bible study works exceptionally for me. I believe I do not require the opinions of a lot of others for what His purpose is for me. It does not mean that the counsel of others is never relevant, only that some very specific alone time is extremely productive for me.

Dive into the Truth, ask the Holy Spirit for wisdom for how this Truth applies to you specifically, and then listen. This method leaves no wiggle room for anything other than becoming aware of His purpose for you.

\* \* \*

The underpinnings of my spiritual self . . . my inner core . . . my soul . . . all find their foundation in the Word. Then my conversation with the Holy Spirit, my Abba Father and my King Jesus are my dream team to start my day. My conversation with each of them is specific to their character and how they show up for me. I truly make it a conversation, and the only other member of my household at this time—my daughter—must think I am crazy, but she's now used to my "outloud" conversations.

"You do not have because you do not ask God. When you ask, you do not receive, because you ask with wrong motives, that you may spend what you get on your pleasures." James 4:2b-3 (NIV)

People tell me all the time that they either never hear God speaking to them or that they find it hard to believe I do. I am not saying that if you were in my living room during my morning conversations with God you would hear Him when I say I hear Him outloud.

I am saying that when you make it a habit of going to the ones who know the beginning through the end, the ones who know how your day will go, you develop the ability to hear their voices above the white noise. They speak to me through the Word. They speak to me through other humans by having them verbalize what they have already shown me in my heart and mind.

You must be grounded in the Truth. The Father, Son and Holy Spirit will never have a calling or purpose for you which goes against the Truth or against their character. You must exercise speaking to and listening to them through the word and in prayer and meditation. I promise you that they hear you and are anxiously waiting for you to spend time with them.

It is definitely asking in the right motives to desire to know what God's purpose is for you. Trust me when I say that doing what is right in your own eyes is not a good strategy. The number of times I have had to "re-take" life tests is staggering. My prayer for you would be that exactly what you receive from my words is that you make a habit of seeking the Lord every day before you hear any other voice.

Ask the Holy Spirit to help you hear Him. Ask to see the healing. Ask for healing. Ask for the ability to forgive. Ask for forgiveness. Ask for the courage and strength to do the challenging work which begins the healing journey. He will answer in unexpected ways, so do not put your expectations on Him. It will be beyond what you could ask or imagine. Stand in awe.

\* \* \*

I am a voracious reader, specifically of nonfiction. I read the autobiographies of heroes of the faith, as well as some great Christian writers. I resonate with authors who have walked a similar path and come through the fire on the other side. We have all had some brokenness in our lives. We have all failed others and have had others fail us. Ultimately, we need our expectations to only be in the One who never fails.

My favorite authors remind me of this truth and speak of their steps of healing. Over the years, I have consumed many books which have helped me see how I have been surviving the trauma in my life. Several since my divorce have had an impact not only on that trauma but on the trauma of my childhood as well.

*Uninvited* by Lysa TerKeurst had been in the many stacks of unread books around my house prior to my divorce, and I thought it covered something very different. I cannot begin to describe what it has meant to me regarding my complete and total lack of discernment in my choices of relationships as I have grown from adolescence to adulthood.

The things I shut down and repressed due to the wounds I received as a child were being spilled out on the pages in front of me as if she had plugged a thumb drive into my soul. I know that is why she writes. Her King has called her to comfort other people with the comfort she has received.

Lysa's public walk through childhood rejection and marriage infidelity mirror my own and make me feel a bond with a sister in Christ. Women, and frankly humans, need to know they have safe places to talk about what they have been through without judgement.

I have no doubt that some of what I have said here will receive "opinions." I know my Savior and King have called me to tell my story, and I am obedient. I have added books Lysa has recommended, along with others by my favorite authors, to be companions to my inductive Bible studies and indeed feel my preparations for my King bearing fruit.

\* \* \*

My morning meditation and quiet time are a non-negotiable aspect of my spiritual healing. No one else is up in my house, and copious amounts of coffee are involved. I have an extensive prayer list, as well as time of "hashing out" what I am doing well and what can use a little work. It sets the stage for the day, and I never walk out of a reflective session feeling anything but encouraged and lifted. As a believer, going to my Creator, who knows the beginning from the end, as well as His creation inside and out, is the only thing that makes sense for me to "be not anxious" about anything.

All these aspects of my spiritual health make for a daily touch of my King's hand on all that I do. Do I always get it right? Cannot stop laughing. I inevitably put my own finger-prints on things and muck it up . . . but when I swing back around . . . my King gently welcomes me home and shows me extravagant grace. Grace that gives me peace and calms my anxious soul. Frankly, that is all I need.

As a believer, there is no healing of the wounds I have re-ceived without the Holy Spirit. This relationship binds all the other areas of my life together to make for a holistic healing of the wounds and an understanding of how to continue my healing journey at all.

If life happens and I end up heading out for the day and miss any component of my morning routine, it shows the rest of the day. The day isn't a disaster, it just tends to lack the focus and the energy I need to interact with myself and others in a meaningful way. If I skip my usual morning spiritual practices, I have to make an effort not to allow my mental and emotional energy to vomit on everyone because I didn't choose to abide in the energy of the power which raised Christ from the dead.

I cannot recall the last time I allowed my morning to start without the board meeting of my Abba Father, my King Jesus, and the Holy Spirit. It is vitally important to the ongoing healing and health of the wounds I have received and to my growth as the woman God intended me to be. The closer I grow to Them and the longer I listen to Their voices, the easier it becomes to know for a fact that I am hearing Their will and purpose for my life.

The spiritual section of the Outloud Healing Companion includes exercises in gratitude, as well as how to have a conversation with Abba Father, King Jesus, and the Holy Spirit and begin your healing journey hearing Their voice.

# Chapter 13

## Know Your Worth

---

"Your value doesn't decrease based on someone's
inability to see your worth."

*–Zig Ziglar*

---

Riding high with my college degree in hand in May of 2017, it was time to seek gainful employment. I am not one to lump humans into groups; however, there was a bit of ageism by the younger interviewers as I headed out. I get that it can be a quandary. Do you look at a mature applicant as stable because they stayed at a handful of jobs for a long time? Or do you look at them as on the downhill slide and figure they won't stick around long in the position?

I was watching twenty-somethings get handed tech jobs paying $80–100K right out of college with their degree. I came with a degree and forty plus years of experience and was being treated like I was a mummy. Even though I chose not to put dates on my résumé, the sheer volume of experience belied at least a bit of maturity, as I passed my résumé along the job market gauntlet.

I confess that some imposter syndrome was present, since I did not believe I was proficient at every detail in each job description. When I was in my twenties, I would go on interviews for jobs I was half-qualified for and convince the employers I was their gal. If I did not have confidence in me, why should they?

After uploading dozens of résumés and going on a handful of interviews, I was about to accept a position which would not pay me a salary commensurate with my degree or experience, just so I would have a job. Then, my Jesus set up a divine appointment for me. I was driving home from dropping Maya off at school, and I got a call from someone who had my résumé show up in their Indeed inbox as a candidate for a job they posted.

We were both caught off-guard, since I had not sought or even seen the posting for this position, and he had not removed the ad from its previous filling. There was Jesus. The pay was not what my younger counterparts were receiving, but it was acceptable. The job also came with a four-day workweek when tax season was over, so an eight-month stint of three-day weekends sounded like a great benny. The work rewarded my intuitive and critical thinking skills and got me incremental pay increases for the skills and abilities I acquired along the way.

I have never considered myself stupid, but I am not a genius either. I do believe I am capable of some God-given discernment and have put that to good use in more recent years. I wish I had acknowledged said discernment during the endgame of my marriage, but alas it is over and cannot be lamented. Time to move forward and make intelligent, informed decisions.

I feel I am doing that in all areas of my life. I am trying to be a good steward of my money and preparations for the future. I go over my bills and expenses quarterly to make sure I am not overspending or underachieving. I have only so many years of receiving money from my alimony and business remuneration, and I want to make the best use of these resources.

I am applying good judgement to my health and any need for resources going forward, should it take a turn for the worse. I have items in place which would not require me to be married to someone or need Maya to sacrifice in case I need care or if something catastrophic happens to me.

I had not thought through what resources I didn't have before I ended my marriage. Again, I was thinking through the lens of emotions. I hope you would never have to go through a divorce. But should you, please take some time to think of your exit strategy. If you have no money of your own and no place to go, unless you are being physically abused, get those things even a little in order and then move forward.

A schedule was now established, and my anxiety and decision fatigue regarding provision were abating. This allowed me to focus on the other areas of my life to begin healing in earnest.

\* \* \*

I am now wading neck-deep into the process of "dating". I make it sound like some kind of chore, when in fact it has been a blast. It is like an amusement park and a long episode of *CSI: Crime Scene Investigation*. I was foolhardy enough to think I knew what I was getting myself into. The rumors about the zoo which is the dating app scene are not exaggerated.

As the geeky little researcher that I am, I of course looked into all sorts of apps, meetup groups, singles groups through church, and several other online possibilities. Sadly, even the ones which claim to take a Christian stance have defined "Christian" differently than my King Jesus. I also had to discover that nothing about this process was like the last time I had dated almost thirty years ago.

You must be sharp and keep your critical thinking skills and wits about you. You will need to do some detective work and be prepared to know you will be asked things you may not want to flippantly answer. You do want to be truthful, but everyone doesn't need to know your whole life on the first date or conversation.

Not long into this adventure, I realized I was clueless. I have learned and been taught by my circumstances as well as by the gentlemen I have encountered along the way. There have been a few occasions where I cannot even begin to describe here the things they said to me or sent to me. For the most part, it has been educational and so much fun. The opportunity to meet and have conversations with intelligent adult males has been more entertaining than I could have ever imagined.

As I walked through the fire of discerning what knowledge and wisdom I actually needed to move forward in my journey, and what was merely other people's opinions and random advice, I felt as if I tapped into a part of my mind which was a new frontier.

All of these thoughts either ran through my head as I was filling out my dating profiles or were immediately encountered as the games began. You need to truly understand yourself. Where are you in life in regard to your physical and financial health? What do you expect of someone you would meet? What do you bring to the table?

Some things seemed like common sense to me. Others are apparently not to the general public. My "wisdom" on the subject of dating was that you were allowed to be looking for someone who was representative of what you brought to the relationship. Healthy lifestyle, not a lot of debt, similar season of life, etc . . . Boy, was I in for a surprise.

The first thing you need to get a mental grasp of is that there is no absolute truth on dating sites. I mean, I was on them and knew I was telling the truth, so I am sure there are others who are equally honest. But after a couple years into this process, it was like looking for the holy grail out there. It would have been easier for me to get the nuclear launch codes than to find a man who meant all of what he said in his bio.

Many people I knew had met and married wonderful people they met on dating sites. Many others said I should trust the process. Where does someone who is in their late-fifties organically meet people? And being a Christian and not wanting to hook up with random men for the rest of my life seemed to be shocking to other self-proclaimed Christians on said sites.

\* \* \*

The temporary relationships I allowed myself to enter opened a whole new world of manipulation. Apparently, it is not hard to recognize a wounded, vulnerable human, even in an eight-picture, two hundred-word bio on an internet site. It was definitely hunting season for single, divorced, mature, betrayed individuals who would be presumed to be desperate to give over all of themselves, as opposed to being alone.

I thought I knew my identity and what I genuinely believed about myself. I discovered very quickly that my love language—words of affirmation—could be used against me. When you have been lied to your whole life, you set the stage for the lovely lies you want to believe about yourself to be true.

Imposter syndrome is an interesting term which refers to a psychological experience characterized by persistent self-doubt and the inability to internalize one's achievements, despite verifiable evidence of competence. It is easier to apply this concept to measurable skills and achievements. When it comes to relationships and not doubting the value you bring to the table, it is another matter altogether.

It boggles my mind and breaks my heart that I struggle to believe my good qualities and character traits, while I allow other people to manipulate me to take advantage of them. In reality, the unhealthy attention of someone who knows how to speak to those wounds in my life is a "me" problem, not a "he" problem. Don't get me wrong, men are not being kind by using me in this way, but I have been so desperate to have someone seek me that I have taught each and every one of them that I am receptive to this behavior.

I found myself in a conversation with the Holy Spirit about why my mind works the way it does. The way certain thoughts come to mind, ones which are horrible and have no basis in reality. Thoughts about how people will talk to me or react to me when going into unknown situations. Thoughts connected to individuals whom I made the choice to engage with and now cannot get them or our activity out of my mind.

As I was asking Him why this happens and how to abate them or at least have some type of bulwark set up, He very clearly gave me the words and I spoke them outloud: *This is how you see yourself.*

I am projecting onto others what I find inadequate about myself. Thus, preemptively preparing myself for their rejection.

This made my isolating behavior more palatable than actually taking a hard look at myself and healing or course-correcting.

However, it is much harder to explain away the uncomfortable truth that I am the common denominator regarding the lack of or the type of relationships I have. After all, according to motivational speaker Jim Rohn, we are the "average of the five people we spend the most time with," right?

Unless I have a split personality or I include the Prime delivery guy, I wasn't allowing five people in on the conversation. The Holy Spirit, my King Jesus, and my Abba Father were enough. Alone was where they wanted me. I needed to genuinely see what the workload was and how to proceed.

# Chapter 14

## It's All in Your Head

---

"There's no such thing as a handicap –
it's all in your head."

*–Beverly Hamilton*

---

Of course, it is in your head. Every action and activity is run through our nervous system, and mission control is our brain. Sixty thousand thoughts a day. Ninety-five percent are repeats, and seventy-five percent are negative. The more times you think a thought, the stronger the neuropathway becomes, and it becomes a stronghold.

Can you stop the thoughts? Maybe not. What can you do to keep them from landing or sticking around? You can take them captive. You can preempt those thoughts with the truth. Saturate your thoughts with the Word of God. Have a scripture ready to take the sword of truth to those lies and strike them down. Speaking the Word of God outloud. Processing lies and anxiety has to be taken through the logical lens of the Truth of God. Not the world, not your friends' opinions. Listen to the vertical voices from above and manage the brain God gave you.

After one visit to my gym, the young man who is the manager commented as I was leaving, "Done already?" Two little words. Did he even know my name? He absolutely didn't know my age, health, or goals. For months after this, every time I went to the gym those words would pop into my head. I knew what I was doing and what I wanted to accomplish.

Our bodies don't know the difference when we make disparaging remarks about ourselves or have a negative focus. Every visit to the gym may have been a waste to some degree because I allowed my mental clarity to be clouded.

The reality was that I knew I could push myself harder but wasn't. I was accomplishing my goals, so pushing harder wasn't even necessary, per se, but those two little words were whispering that I wasn't doing enough.

Understanding that I was projecting on to that young man my own feelings of never being enough was a load that wasn't his to carry. I was doing this in every area of my life. I was an imposter. Sixty-two years old and not one single one of my intimate relationships was a success.

I hadn't prayed about entering any of those relationships. I didn't discuss with my King whether they were divine appointments or my lustful desires. This does not absolve the men of their behaviors: lying, cheating, and rejecting. However, I have to own that they were behaving as they always had and had from the beginning. Not excuses, only reasons.

Once again, I was being shown how my lack of healing created a disconnect between my thinking and feeling regarding my life choices. I was allowing how I felt to dictate my identity and what I was worth. I was devaluing who I was in Christ and therefore selling myself to the lowest bidder.

We cannot find healing in any area while neglecting all the others. They were beautifully created and intricately intertwined. Of the top five toxins in our world, anxiety is a chart-topper. If left unchecked, it can cause more damage to our bodies than sugar or alcohol. Anxiety starts its damage by wreaking havoc on our sleep cycle. After that, a cascade of system damage begins to take place. It is possible to recover from this type of damage; however, it will take a lot of hard work.

In my frustration regarding the battle of my mind, I cried out to the Holy Spirit as to how I am supposed to keep the lies out of my head. Is there even a way to keep them from cropping up in the first place? Once they do, why does the damage last so long, like the blast from a hand grenade?

What we have experienced and what we have allowed to enter our hearts and minds will not be erased. There will be things that happen, good and bad, which bring up past experiences. The question isn't really how to stop them, although I believe we can exercise our brains to be the bouncers and keep these thoughts and memories from rising to consciousness.

We can allow the Holy Spirit to bring wisdom and understanding of how to take the power we have given those thoughts and plug it in where growth and wisdom in our thinking can bear fruit in line with having the mind of Christ.

With some of the battles, I have been the one who went looking for experiences and conversations which were not healthy but somehow gave me the illusion of positive attention and reduced feelings of loneliness. For this, I cannot blame any abuser; I have to own my own behavior. I have to relinquish the stronghold to the Holy Spirit to further the process of renewing my mind with experiences and thoughts which give me peace in whatever season the Lord has me.

First and foremost, I have to be content with being alone with my Jesus. Not thinking that any relationship will replace those thoughts, and in fact could be more harmful if I am not healing. Then and only then will I acquire the discernment to both have relationships and be the kind of relationship my King has in mind.

As I wrestle with the battles in my heart and mind, I realize the thoughts I have are irrelevant to reality. Conjuring up what could happen is a fool's errand. Even as I justify and convince myself that my logic is sound, the truth is there are a thousand things that "could happen." The decision fatigue and mental gymnastics I go through are only causing me to feel my anxiety doubled.

I not only go through the potential of some evil possibilities, I could then go through the actuality. Which would justify my thinking. In the worst-case scenario, none of the things I dread ever happen, and I have frittered away time, breath, health, and mental soundness while trying to avoid what is not real.

My homework with the Holy Spirit is not only to firm up the bulwark of my mind but also to know what to do with those thoughts when they come and not allow them to wreak havoc on all my systems. Just because my Creator will not interfere with the free will of his creation does not mean His protection for me is out of reach.

If we listen closely to what the Holy Spirit has to say daily—and He will speak every day—we can genuinely take those thoughts captive. We can know what to do with them to contain the fallout and eventually give them no oxygen to show up in the first place.

Typically, the physical decisions come first and are a tad easier. But these, too, are mental choices to see what is happening and create a routine and plan to take back what has been damaged or lost.

Anxiety is tricky, since there are good and bad reasons for our reactions to it. Go on a first date—good anxiousness. Lose your job—bad anxiousness. Our mind and body don't know the difference out of the gate. So we need to take a breath, look at what is real and what is true, and then decide if we need to channel the good energy into preparing for a first date or release the provision of the next job into the Lord's hands.

\*\*\*

Each year, a dear friend of mine challenges me to discover what my word for that year would be. It is not meant to be flippant or to be a contest to judge the popularity of the word. The choice involves truly praying about and deciding on a word which would encompass a lot of what my path would include for that year.

When I talk about a "word" for the year I am not merely talking about having a kitschy phrase. While we are not shown all of the details of our purpose in one setting, we are given our calling and purpose as more of an overview. In the fall of each year, I begin praying about what the coming year will hold and what my additional purpose will be.

My word encompasses how I am to approach my purpose. What I am to meditate on. I go back to it over and over when I want to renew my mind and stave off unwanted thoughts or when I am struggling with decisions.

I have loved the journey with each and every word my Jesus has given me. "Alone" and

"Journey" have been prominent and can be seen throughout my story. I love words and especially when they can have a double meaning that is intelligently witty. The Holy Spirit speaks to me this way regularly.

My Abba Father has shown me that I am never alone and that learning to be content when I'm by myself, not in need of anyone or anything else, is not a bad place to be. At least for the time He needs to help me work on healing and growth.

Word for 2016: Alone – separated from others, isolated; exclusive of anyone or anything else; considered without reference to any other; unique–alone among their contemporaries in respect.

I am learning to be comfortable alone. Not in sadness, although some of it is. I believe for the Lord to teach me that I am never truly alone. Also, to learn that He, alone, is truly enough. Interestingly, I find myself in an "alone" season as I am putting the finishing touches on this book and walking through the trials the Lord would have me learn from to move on to "forever."

"My soul finds rest in God alone; my salvation comes from him. He alone is my rock and my salvation; he is my fortress, I will never be shaken." Psalm 62:2 (NIV)

Word for 2017: Journey – an act of traveling from one place to another; a long and often difficult process of personal change and development; travel somewhere; a day's work; daily portion.

I love all the meanings. I do believe I will be traveling from one place to another and my journey will be a difficult process of personal change and development as I submit to the authority of my Lord. Through it all, the Lord will be my daily portion as I travel somewhere. The full weight of this book and its purpose have to do with my "journey." Thus the tagline, "It's the Journey." It is my mantra, my hashtag, and my life.

I sincerely believe life is all about the journey and not the ultimate destination. Although knowing our ultimate destination could not be more crucial to the journey. I know who my savior is and where I will spend eternity . . . thus the journey has so much more meaning than simply getting to that destination.

"For he will command his angels concerning you to guard you in all your ways." Psalm 91:11 (NIV)

\* \* \*

As I am walking my healing journey, I have integrated many things into the healing of my mind. I read some white papers on the research for a company called Smart Fit which speaks about the activity that best regenerates our brain cells. We have about a week as a window to take action to help our newly developing brain cells to integrate into our brain and the synaptic connections. If we do nothing, or actually do things which are toxic to our brain cells, we miss out on an opportunity.

On the other hand, if we add a process to our schedule which incorporates some physical activity with a mental one, we capitalize on an opportunity.

If we are performing some physical activity and incorporate something mental, e.g., dribbling a basketball while doing math problems, we can help our brains recover from injury and take advantage of the regeneration window. This process has been instrumental in helping individuals with traumatic brain injuries, concussions, Alzheimer's disease, and developmental disabilities.

At age sixty-two, I am not showing signs of memory loss or any condition affecting my mind or brain. I have, however, over my lifetime, done things which have, in fact, killed off a few brain cells.

As part of my mental healing journey, these are some of the ways in which I am incorporating this philosophy:

- Jigsaw puzzles: it is a physical activity in that you are typically standing, as well as moving to choose and place the pieces. This is mental in the pairing the space with the piece that belongs there. I know it sounds simple, but it is a great start, and it replaces mindless scrolling as well.

- Exercise & Memorization: I work out three times a week, and when the sun is out, I walk a couple times a week as well. I utilize my mind in focusing on the proper form and outcomes of these exercises. I also use scripture memorization. This brings me peace and alleviates any anxiety about what I need to do later in the day, along with staying in the moment of the positive outcome of the exercise.

One hundred percent of the God of the universe is within us as believers. We have the mind of Christ. The Holy Spirit is the deliverer of the understanding of the things of God. When I am in the middle of His will, the most precious healing takes place.

\* \* \*

Being intentional about what comes into my mind through the gateways of my eyes and ears, just as with my specific efforts to "detox" my body by watching what I eat and put on my skin, I need to be a gatekeeper of what comes into my mind and decides to stick around.

I chose to cancel DirectTV and be more intentional with any programming choices to stream. I feel the same about music and podcasts as well. I know a lot of people think it is ridiculous to take music lyrics seriously or to be concerned with the amount of foul language any show contains.

It is scientifically proven that when thoughts go through our brain repeatedly, they become strongholds. Our brain doesn't have a bouncer to sort out if a thought is serious or not. It also doesn't matter if the stimulus is visual and audio from some program or from something we are reading. We are taking it in, and our mind is doing something with it.

Acknowledging that thoughts will come as long as my brain is functioning. What I do with them—both to abate their impact and to set up a bulwark around what I do wish to focus on—is the stronghold I set up for myself.

We don't need to sit in sackcloth and ashes and read scriptures all day; however, repentance, forgiveness, and scripture-reading are integral to finding, beginning, and moving forward in healing.

The people you have around you are not only with you for spiritual and emotional connections. Have wise counsel around you. Individuals who are learning and growing and holding you accountable are equally important to your overall healing and well-being.

The other day, I heard something on a podcast I thought was interesting. The gentleman said you can tell who is in your child's ear by their actions and reactions. Are they listening to you and your counsel as a parent, or listening to their friends who have not yet matured enough to be giving advice?

I joke that for me to find a mentor who is close to my age and experience, I might need to hold a séance or to find a mummy. In fact, someone who could speak into my ear and hold me accountable and be part of the cheering section for my growth and learning could be any age.

Some people in my age range act as if they are on the downhill slide and merely waiting for death. The Lord told me to start a podcast to further my story, and I started that at sixty. He asked me to write a book, and the first one was published when I was sixty-two. I pride myself in looking for something new to learn every day. Even if it is the definition of a word I see in a game app I play.

There is a saying out there about being 1% better each day. Not swinging for 100% every day and then berating yourself when the inevitable failure happens. Consistently improving by small habits leads to incredible progress and a fulfilling life.

The mental section of the Outloud Healing Companion walks you through your routines and the types of steps you can take each day to strive for mental wellness and the 1% improvement.

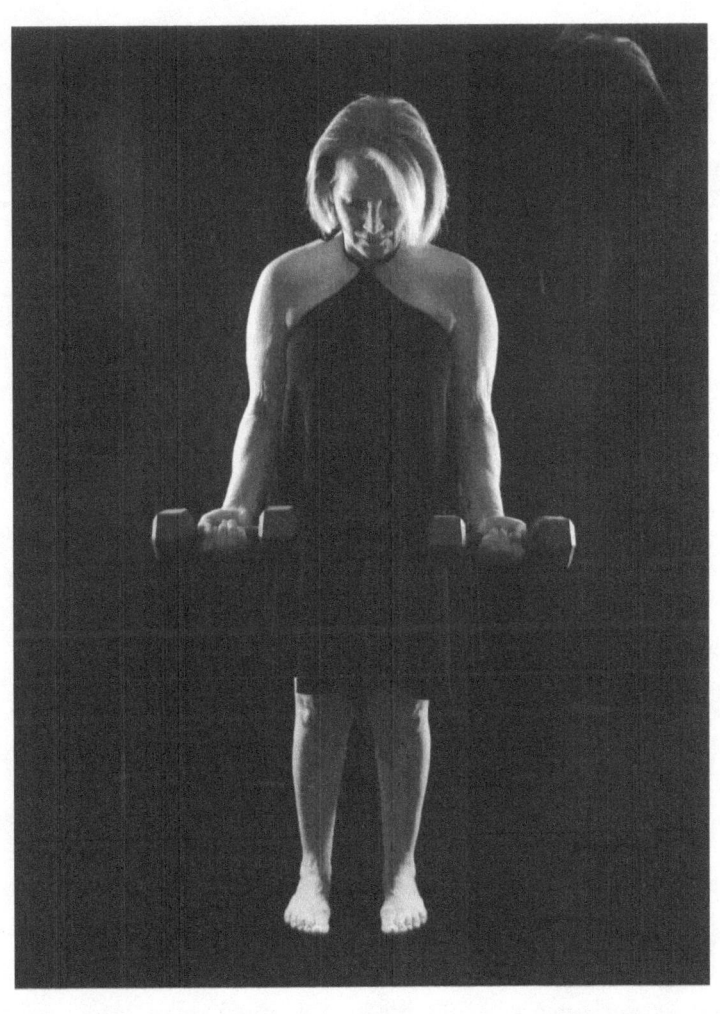

# Chapter 15

## In the Mirror

---

"When you look in the mirror, remember the battles
you've won, and the strength you've gained."

*–Maya Angelou*

---

My overall health at the time of my divorce was unstable at best. In recent years, I had had a better handle on my physical health, but the chaos of the separation and ensuing divorce brought a whole host of things I was unsure of how to deal with. As with every situation in my life, I dove into research headfirst.

I had been battling my weight throughout menopause. Ray's infidelity and rejection of me during this time, including intimacy, did not bolster my love for or belief in myself in the slightest. The first step in my healing was the Lord reminding me whose I was. Reminding me where I get my worth and identity.

The fact is, even when I had successes physically—and some were impressive—Ray was no longer on my team and therefore showed me no appreciation for the effort. I had to learn to release the need for anyone else to approve of me or my appearance. I needed to be a good steward of the health and abilities the Holy Spirit gave me to fulfill my purpose. Period.

I had been walking with a friend two to three times a week when the divorce began. While battling hormonal imbalances due to menopause, it did not seem like walking was helping my body composition or health. But it only seemed that way to me. It is funny how we can't, or maybe don't, see when we are making genuine positive change because we are still looking at ourselves with the vision others cast on us.

\* \* \*

It all came to a head in August of 2018 when my mom passed away, and it appears my menopause came to a full stop. My initial weight loss came as the result of my concerns about some nefarious circumstances surrounding my mom's death. Later in life, I have tended to be a stress non-eater, and this could cause a weight loss which may or may not be of the type of body material I wished . . . i.e., fat.

I do not recommend this as your launching pad, but it was effective for me in dropping the first twelve pounds and causing the sudden appearance of an increased metabolism I hadn't had even during my bodybuilding years. This, along with some unusual friendships which gave me back some belief in what was possible and specifically what I was capable of, became the start of the physical portion of my preparations for my king.

I did absolutely nothing on this journey for a specific man

or even the hope of one. I did it all to become the woman God created me to be and who is beautifully and wonderfully made. When people talk about being good stewards, I have never believed that meant only money. I believe we are being instructed to be good stewards of all God has given us. Our time, money, talents, health, possessions . . . all of it. If I am physically able, I am instructed to serve and to GO.

Frankly, even with the extra weight, I was healthy. I have never been on medication and have always been able to serve in ministry. I just felt that allowing myself to keep the additional weight would eventually become a hindrance to my physical abilities. I wasn't going to waste other resources by paying to have weight-loss surgery or anything, not that I am judging people who choose that avenue. At that point, I decided I hadn't exhausted all avenues available from my Creator, even though sometimes it felt like I had.

So, I am down twelve pounds. A man I was talking to online was encouraging me as a woman and in general as a human being with his own positive motivation. I have never met him. He may not even be real. But his words meant a lot to me and helped me to take the steps to start on this physical transformation journey.

Again, I did not do any of this for a specific man or hope of one. He was simply encouraging. My dear friend Holli was also very encouraging. We had been walking and hiking together for several years, and she had recently moved to a home near me, so we were on a regular schedule. I decided to see what she had done to drop over fifty pounds over the last year.

She had done a low-carb, no-sugar kind of ketogenic diet of her own. My bodybuilding years had taught me some other things regarding calories, macro nutrients, and muscle. I decided to check out the keto thought process and even used a macro calculator to see what food would look like for me should I choose the keto lane. Feeling motivated by my initial weight loss made letting go of some of the carbs I had left in my life a little easier.

I was older—post-menopause—and had yo-yo dieted since giving birth eighteen years earlier. I had finalized my divorce from a cheating husband, and he had re-married. My only child had graduated high school and would be heading to college. I had graduated with my bachelor's degree and recently started a new job. My mother had passed away, and I had to reconcile unspoken conversations. On the list of stressful life events, I was topping out.

The bigger picture for me is that I knew I needed to make physical changes in the process of preparing for my King. I wanted first and foremost to be a good steward of all the gifts, talents, and abilities I was given and not sit back and think—since I knew I was headed to eternity with my King—that I didn't have a purpose to fulfill. And I wanted to share my life with someone, which would require that I get my head, heart, mind, and body on their healing journey.

\* \* \*

When I was younger, in my twenties, I competed in bodybuilding and did so naturally. I worked hard because I had to. I did not have a naturally occurring, high-functioning metabolism. Probably from years of caffeine abuse, among other things, and various dieting. At this time, there was every diet and nutrition concept known to man floating around.

Back then, I had the benefit of a couple professional bodybuilders guiding me and training me. Their basic thought process was that I was not consuming enough protein, or calories for that matter, and I was encouraged to eat more. This was foreign to me, since society at large told women to eat next to nothing and especially not more protein, as it would make us look like men.

After the first month of upping my consumption of calories and protein, I looked totally transformed. I do not say this lightly, as I have NEVER been someone to speak highly of myself in any arena. I was not muscled enough to compete yet, but body fat had departed, and the right kind of curves were leading and following me into a room.

I worked out and built muscle and finally decided to compete in bodybuilding. In my twenties, I competed twice. The first time, there were over thirty women in my weight class. I had gotten the stomach flu the week before the competition and lost weight I could not afford to lose and looked flat. I placed 9th though and felt good about it as my first competition. For my second competition, they combined the middleweight and heavyweight classes, and I took 3rd against two heavyweights.

Over the years since bodybuilding, I did various things to either lose or maintain weight. Having a baby and miscarriages, going through menopause, and frankly dealing with the stresses of life made the process exciting, to say the least. When my divorce started, I weighed more than I wanted, and the stress not only made it difficult to lose the extra pounds but also caused me to clench my jaw, and I now had braces on to fix my bite. This was a high school nightmare coming to life.

I tried everything I knew which had worked previously. Even after eliminating troublesome food groups and adding the appropriate exercise for me and my body type, I could not gain or lose a pound. It was not only frustrating, it was also disheartening. To be honest, I was feeling resigned to being overweight. This is not my nature. I feel at heart like I am an encourager and never lose hope. Probably why I stayed in my marriage so long after it was obvious that I was the only one trying.

Walking is one of the best things you can do for your overall health, and I was reaping the benefits whether I realized it or not. I openly admit that when I was walking with my friend, our conversations often devolved into talk about the divorce and kind of sat in a low-level negativity. This was not good for my anxiety or other areas of my mental health and was definitely counterproductive.

Funnily enough, a move on her part to much farther away and then the Covid lockdowns created an environment where I had to walk by myself. The Holy Spirit had me right where he wanted me. I began to use my solitary walks as a prayer and gratitude time. Or sometimes just being quiet and allowing Him to give me my marching orders.

\* \* \*

I was down thirty pounds now and my braces came off, so my promise to my daughter to get "back in the game" had to have boots on the ground. Filling out profiles on dating apps is like playing "truth or dare." The first couple of apps I chose made me put up six to eight pictures and either demanded or suggested that at least one be full-body. It was comical how many guys in my age range posted their high school sports picture. Even if the other pictures were more current, I didn't understand the thought process. I could have put my bodybuilding pictures from my twenties, but I figured people would say, "What the hell happened to her?"

The profile questions having to do with physical measurements were vague to begin with, but the fact that people would lie about their height or body type boggled my mind. We would all be meeting one another at some point; did they really think their deception would get by everyone unnoticed?

In all fairness, the body type choices were not very succinct either. But seriously, marking "athletic" when you are fifty to a hundred pounds overweight has to prick your conscience sometime before you upload the profile. The same holds true for height. If you claim to be six feet tall and then post a full-body picture near a doorway—well, we can see the reality.

I take great care of my skin, and with my new-found weight loss, I looked younger than my age. I do not believe that was totally a factor in why so many younger guys were reaching out to me, but I was informed that if they desired "mature" women, it didn't hurt if they looked good.

Coming out of my marriage feeling neglected, rejected, and very raw and open to affirmation that I looked good and was desirable made for a perfect storm. My unhealed wounds yearned for the balm of being found attractive and being desired. Diving into dating and establishing physical contact was a spark that started a blaze which created new wounds at my own hands that are still being tended.

The bonds that are established and the unspoken promises that are made when you have a physical connection in a relationship are not to be underestimated. I justified my choices and convinced myself that I deserved the attention and that because I had been neglected, I could do this to somehow establish some kind of self-worth. The problem is, I never had any self-worth to begin with.

Every single intimate male relationship I had ever had began with a physical connection. I believed any connection was acceptable because I knew who I was and I was in control of how long it would last and that it wasn't for forever. Not one of the men genuinely knew me or valued me. It was what I had fastened my worth to, and they did not flinch at seeing my value through the same lens.

This went against every single thing I was being shown by the Holy Spirit as healthy and as my identity as a daughter of the King. While I am being walked through the fire, the Holy Spirit is lavishing on me the grace and wisdom to understand how much I mean to my Abba Father and how to establish boundaries which protect all of who I am so genuine healing can literally make me feel safe.

# Chapter 16

## It's All About the Math

---

"Numbers don't lie, people do."

*–Ernie Lindsey*

---

I have gone to a naturopathic doctor for over twenty five years, and prior to that I didn't go to any doctors with the exception of my women's annual exam. Dr O'Brien fastidiously keeps records and has this chart tracking my lab work, among other things. Her questions are always holistic in nature and cover how everything impacts us as a whole—emotionally, spiritually, mentally, and physically.

On this visit, I had no particular issue to discuss, and we were only going to go over my annual labs. Or so we thought.

I know it will shock you to hear that I am not a perfect physical specimen. I do have things I would like to be different, and I have always prided myself on doing my research and working things out with regard to sleep, diet, exercise, and supplementation, if necessary.

I had lost all that weight after my mother's passing and decided it was a bridge too far. I swung the pendulum back a bit, and now it was swinging in a direction I hadn't planned. The science geek in me was going to find out why.

The unrealistic fears and emotions I was feeling through the divorce—being by myself and then having my daughter move out—led me to the conclusion that my struggle with mental health had to do with some hiccups in my sleep cycle and therefore was a cortisol balance and anxiety issue.

My doctor was pointing out the parts of my lab work which were sending up flares. Because of her handy-dandy chart, we could see which results had consistently been in the same range and those which were rearing their heads. Several markers pointed toward inflammation and perhaps some kind of viral undertone.

It was tax season, and I was not drinking any alcohol. I was a "ketovore"—living a low-carb lifestyle between ketogenic and carnivore—and was eating whole foods and cooking at home to eliminate toxins and bad oils. I had moved to raw dairy and literally felt less "puffy" from the inside out. It puzzled me that I would still have inflammatory markers.

As we began to discuss my sleep issues, which I of course had already self-diagnosed, I told more of my personal story to my doctor. She tilted her head and calmly, as if pointing out an obvious observation, said, "You have lived with some level of fear all your life."

This caused me to begin an uncontrollable ugly cry. The idea was right in front of my face. Yet saying it outloud or phrasing it that way had never occurred to me. I believed at this

139

time that I had been the farthest along in my physical and spiritual healing and that my biggest battlefields were mental and emotional. I was not wrong. I simply needed the reminder that they are all interconnected and actually the healing progresses together.

Fear is cellular. It releases a host of hormones and chemicals and impacts everything starting with our brain and nervous system. My entire body had been in fight-or-flight mode my whole life. I sat with this revelation for the remainder of the weekend and do not have words for how my whole body felt at the revelation and verbalization of my situation.

My King Jesus called me to write my story. He gave me the story, title, cover, timeline, and everything. When I sat down to get out the first draft of *Butterfly Stitches* only for myself, it came out in seasons of time and divided by emotional, spiritual, mental, and physical sections. My Creator was showing me the importance of each of these areas and how they are intricately woven together and interdependent. The healing will not progress if we neglect something.

The Holy Spirit had been giving me what was necessary to heal all along. As my King was asking me to tell my story and continue my healing by showing me it was happening whether I was aware of it or not, my physical wounds would be the first to react. Our hearts, souls, and minds are protected and either healed or further wounded by what we do to our bodies.

While we walk by faith, having the vision of seeing my healing journey take form in my physical body was a salve for my heart, soul, and mind which would keep me pressing into my Savior in anticipation of the remainder of the trip.

* * *

Healing physically requires an understanding of where you

stand currently. I know none of the preventive tests and lab work sound like fun, nor does weighing, measuring, or looking at yourself naked in a mirror. These are not things you do for appearance's sake only. Taking advantage of your free preventive tests included with most health insurance policies is a great place to start and establish a baseline.

Each year, I get my women's annual exam which comes with referrals for other tests at intervals. A colonoscopy is only required first at age fifty and then at five- to ten-year intervals depending on other factors. Twice, I had a mammogram pop one of my breast implants, and I now do thermograms, which are even better for more diagnostics, as opposed to mammograms.

A lot of professionals are now publishing research which shows that lab work can be based on the "normal" of our current population, not "normal" of an optimal health scenario. Until the labs change these criteria, we can simply go into these tests well-informed and have someone interpreting them who has that experience as well.

Since I knew where I stood when I lost the initial weight after my mother's passing, I felt good about making further changes in the direction of a ketogenic, low-carb lifestyle. Once I knew what that looked like on a plate, I did not have to measure it out every time. It was not a slog, and I felt good and like I was having my "pipes" cleaned out.

Walking continued to be a staple, not only for the physical health benefits, but also for holistic benefits of getting sunshine, breathing fresh air, and being out in creation where I can hear from the Holy Spirit.

All of this helped me lose weight and bring down inflammation. The amount of weight isn't as relevant to my story as letting you know that everyone is different, and you have to do—within the logic of biology and science—what works as a lifestyle for you.

Looking good and feeling healthy snowballed into good sleep and a positive, grateful attitude, which couldn't help but have a positive impact on all the other areas of my life. I chose to add the things we can do for ourselves physically that can have an impact on anxiety or unhealed emotional wounds.

\* \* \*

I had been seeing a lot of research on healing at a cellular level and decided to take a deeper dive. Our body can produce the right amount of any given hormone, but if we have damaged our cells to the point at which they cannot utilize what is produced, a host of conditions can crop up and make it look like we have chronic disease.

I discovered that one of the first things you can do for cellular and mitochondrial health is to detox. Not merely the lovely little box of detox you can get at the health food store, although some of those may be good. I mean, free of charge, start right now, get it out of your life possibilities.

There is so much we can do to be healthier and give ourselves the best assist in healing. It is all a matter of math. Subtract the things which are bad for you. And if you have to ask, it probably is bad for you. I learned that the top five toxins are: Anxiety, alcohol, bad oils, beauty products, and cleaning products. Mind you, there are a plethora of others, but this was a great place to start for me.

No one will ever be one hundred percent toxin-free. But that doesn't mean you can't have a beautiful impact on your healing by doing what you can to lower your toxic load. Doing an audit of not only your physical tests and lab work, but of your environment at home and work, can be incredibly eye-opening.

Taking the bad oils—canola and seed oils—out of my life and cooking mostly at home was not only good for my physical health, but my wallet as well.

Adding the things we are missing or deficient in brings a host of positive side effects with it. As an example, most people are deficient in magnesium and, frankly, minerals in general. I take magnesium in a "sleep stack" at night and physically feel the difference in the other areas a good night's sleep impacts.

The math works so well in helping us get out of the way of ourselves and allows our bodies to work as they were created. Great sleep, plenty of energy, no aches and pains—all these lead to mental, emotional, and spiritual healing as well.

The steps for a triage of each area are included in the Outloud Healing Companion, along with an example of each area's daily routine.

# Scan to order your hard copy of the
## *Outloud Healing Companion* on Amazon

https://a.co/d/gGBnTNW

Or reach out to Michele at: 62michelevrabel@gmail.com with proof of purchase and receive a free PDF download of the *Outloud Healing Companion*

# Epilogue

I do not tell my story to cast blame or to point out the sins of others. They will stand before God on their own to answer for what they did with the life they were given. As will I.

I tell my story to show how what we go through—no matter the cause—shapes us. How it draws us closer to our Creator and develops our character to be who we were designed to be.

I tell my story because it is mine and I own it. I stand before God every morning to press into His heartbeat for me and to live my life to its fullest. To live a life that is full of joy and is in keeping with my purpose.

I do not tell my story to humiliate or run down anyone. I take full accountability for who I was in my relationships and for how long they lasted.

I tell this much of my story to show the wounds of my journey. To show the impact of both the wounds and the healing on my journey.

As with my childhood, if these are the things that I was involved in and aware of and they caused this amount of damage, I shudder to think what happened behind closed doors. Believe me, I do not want to know. My imagination goes down some pretty scary rabbit holes on its own.

The damage done by what actually happened in these relationships has caused wounds that may never fully heal this side of heaven.

The healing is the journey. The healing and my relationship with my Abba Father, King Jesus, and the Holy Spirit are the strongest they have ever been.

The tenderness as I pass over a scar or the sting of a wound still raw shows me how I have grown into the woman They intended.

# Acknowledgments

Every bit of my story was written by my Abba Father, my King Jesus, and my precious Holy Spirit. They are my Board of Directors, and even though it took sixty-three years to genuinely set me on my healing journey, that is where I am firmly planted. The revelations I have been given regarding my identity in Christ—and what genuine loving relationships look like—are priceless. I do not begin a day, make a decision, or react to outside forces without consulting each and every one of them individually.

Maya Victoria, my precious baby girl, was taken along on this journey for better or for worse. If I could take back what she has seen and heard and be the mother and the example God intended all along, I would. But that is not how life goes. Peanut got the momma she was given and has carried herself admirably along her journey. My Comforter has cradled her heart and shown her how to love others well and not judge what she doesn't understand. She is an example of a godly young woman and there is no end to my love for her.

I wish to acknowledge my ex-husband Ray. This is not the story of our marriage. This is not about him. This is my story and about what I went through. I am the one who did not ask my Abba Father if I should be in relationship with Ray, and therefore we did not have a firm foundation as our beginnings. He is not the only reason for our marriage ending. His infidelity is the reason for its ultimate demise. Would we have thrived if the infidelity had stopped? That is speculation, and no one can know. My relationship with Ray was not all bad. The blessing of our daughter definitely brought us many great moments as a family. I have taken ownership of where I have failed our relationship throughout my story and forgiven him for his shortcomings.

Alice, as my editor you deserve a special badge of courage for having to deal with my grammar and punctuation once again. Thank you for your patience and for understanding when I don't change some words because that is just how my feisty gramma actually said it. I don't know if the Lord has more books in store for me and if we will work together again, but thank you for making my first books a memorable experience.

Lindsey, my sweet friend and wonderfully gifted photographer, has once again captured my vision. She knew exactly what to say to draw the emotion and intention of what I wanted to inspire in those who see my book covers. She is a precious sister who has walked a portion of my path and someone I am honored to call my friend for life..

Sweet sisters in Christ who wrote my endorsements and have supported me through Butterfly Stitches and now Outloud, I cannot thank you enough. The support we share with one another as we all are on the journey our King Jesus has asked us to walk has been outstanding.

Michelle, where do I begin with how you have so intricately caught my vision and brought my books to life? Every detail has been exactly as I wanted, even when my explanation was lacking. Your follow-up and encouragement have meant so much to me—I know you deal with a lot of authors—and your way of making me feel as if I am the only one brings me galactic joy.

Sweet friends and family that have bought books, been on launch teams, beta read, and listened when I needed to be outloud, thank you from the bottom of my heart. My cup over-flows and my prayer would be that I could be as inspiring to you in whatever purpose God lays on your heart.

The online universe—what can I say?—there are so many of you that I have not met in person, but who have been some of my biggest cheerleaders. Thank you for loving on me, and I pray I am as big of an encouragement to all of you as you are to me.

# About the Author

Michele Vrabel is the author of *Butterfly Stitches: The Metamorphosis of Healing* and *Outloud: The Sound of Healing*, two powerful memoirs chronicling her journey of healing through emotional, spiritual, mental, and physical restoration. With unflinching honesty and deep faith, Michele invites readers to witness how Jesus met her in the rawest places of her story—transforming her wounds into sacred testimonies of grace.

When she's not writing, Michele serves others through her work as a bookkeeper, offering clarity and order to businesses and ministries alike. She also hosts a soul-nourishing podcast, where she speaks candidly about healing, identity, and what it means to live authentically in God's truth.

Whether on the page, behind the mic, or in everyday spreadsheets, Michele's calling is the same: to help others find freedom in the places they've been silenced and to remind them that healing is not only possible—it's holy.

www.michelevrabel.com
IG: @sweetartbyshelly

# Retreats

**Inside the Chrysalis: metamorphosis begins**

Transformation happens in the hidden, sacred spaces—where stillness replaces striving, and healing begins from the inside out. **Inside the Chrysalis** is a retreat designed to nurture your whole self—**emotionally, mentally, physically, and spiritually**—as you embrace the deep, unseen work of renewal that God is doing within you.

This is a fully **all-inclusive retreat** where your needs are met—**meals, rest, and care are provided**—so that you can focus entirely on your healing journey. Over three days, we will move through the stages of metamorphosis, allowing old wounds to be released, minds to be renewed, bodies to be restored, and spirits to rise in faith.

Visit my website to attend an already-scheduled retreat or to submit a suggestion for a metropolitan area near you.

www.michelevrabel.com

**Scottsdale Retreat**    **Suggest a City**

# Don't Forget to Check Out
## *Butterfly Stiches*

### a memoir PART I

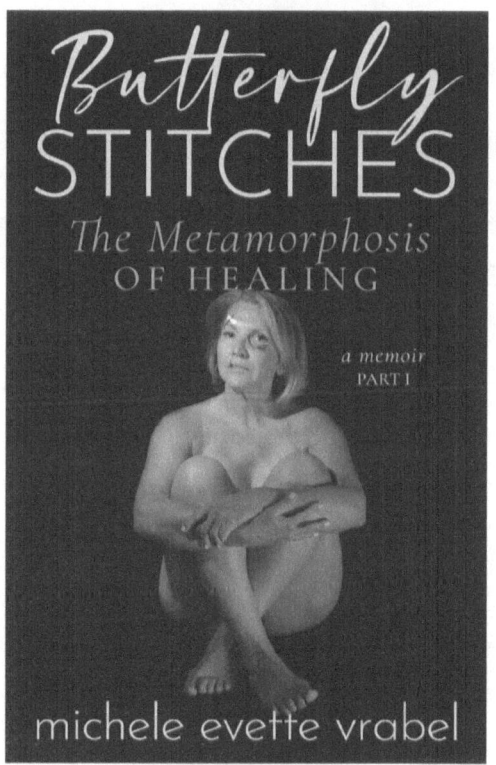

www.ingramcontent.com/pod-product-compliance
Lightning Source LLC
Chambersburg PA
CBHW031529120626
46545CB00005B/2059